PREFACE

Artificial intelligence (AI) may lack an agreed-upon definition, but someone writing about its history must have some kind of definition in mind. For me, artificial intelligence is that activity devoted to making machines intelligent, and intelligence is that quality that enables an entity to function appropriately and with foresight in its environment. According to that definition, lots of things – humans, animals, and some machines – are intelligent. Machines, such as "smart cameras," and many animals are at the primitive end of the extended continuum along which entities with various degrees of intelligence are arrayed. At the other end are humans, who are able to reason, achieve goals, understand and generate language, perceive and respond to sensory inputs, prove mathematical theorems, play challenging games, synthesize and summarize information, create art and music, and even write histories. Because "functioning appropriately and with foresight" requires so many different capabilities, depending on the environment, we actually have several continua of intelligence with no particularly sharp discontinuities in any of them. For these reasons, I take a rather generous view of what constitutes AI. That means that my history of the subject will, at times, include some control engineering, some electrical engineering, some statistics, some linguistics, some logic, and some computer science.

There have been other histories of AI, but time marches on, as has AI, so a new history needs to be written. I have participated in the quest for artificial intelligence for fifty years – all of my professional life and nearly all of the life of the field.

Table of Contents

INTRODUCTION

Since the invention of computers or machines, their capability to perform various tasks went on growing exponentially. Humans have developed the power of computer systems in terms of their diverse working domains, their increasing speed, and reducing size with respect to time.

A branch of Computer Science named Artificial Intelligence pursues creating computers or machines as intelligent as human beings.

In computer science, artificial intelligence (AI), sometimes called machine intelligence, is intelligence demonstrated by machines, in contrast to the natural intelligence displayed by humans. Leading Artificial Intelligence textbooks define the field as the study of "intelligent agents": any device that perceives its environment and takes actions that maximize its chance of successfully achieving its goals. Colloquially, the term "artificial intelligence" is often used to describe machines (or computers) that mimic "cognitive" functions that humans associate with the human mind, such as "learning" and "problem-solving".

As machines become increasingly capable, tasks considered to require "intelligence" are often removed from the definition of Artificial Intelligence, a phenomenon known as the AI effect. A quip in Tesler's Theorem says "AI is whatever hasn't been done yet." For instance, optical character recognition is frequently excluded from things considered to be AI, having become a routine technology. Modern machine capabilities generally classified as AI include successfully understanding human speech, competing at the highest level in strategic game systems (such as chess and Go), autonomously operating cars, intelligent routing in content delivery networks, and military simulations.

Artificial intelligence was founded as an academic discipline in 1956, and in the years since has experienced several waves of optimism, followed by disappointment and the loss of funding (known as an "AI winter"), followed by new approaches, success and renewed funding. For most of its history, AI research has been divided into subfields that often fail to communicate with each other. These sub-fields are based on technical considerations, such as particular goals (e.g. "robotics" or "machine learning"), the use of particular tools ("logic" or artificial neural networks), or deep philosophical differences. Subfields have also been based on social factors (particular institutions or the work of particular researchers).

The traditional problems (or goals) of AI research include reasoning, knowledge representation, planning, learning, natural language processing, perception and the ability to move and manipulate objects. General intelligence is among the field's long-term goals. Approaches include statistical methods, computational intelligence, and traditional symbolic AI. Many tools are used in AI, including versions of search and mathematical optimization, artificial neural networks, and methods based on statistics, probability and economics. The AI field draws upon computer science, information engineering, mathematics, psychology, linguistics, philosophy, and many other fields.

The field was founded on the assumption that human intelligence "can be so precisely described that a machine can be made to simulate it". This raises philosophical arguments about the nature of the mind and the ethics of creating artificial beings endowed with human-like intelligence. These issues have been explored by myth, fiction and philosophy since antiquity. Some people also consider AI to be a danger to humanity if it progresses unabated. Others believe that AI, unlike previous technological revolutions, will create a risk of mass unemployment.

In the twenty-first century, AI techniques have experienced a resurgence following concurrent advances in computer power, large amounts of data, and theoretical understanding; and AI techniques have become an essential part of the technology industry, helping to solve many challenging problems in computer science, software engineering and operations research

What is Artificial Intelligence

Artificial iintelligence (AI) is the simulation of human intelligence processes by machines, especially computer systems. These processes include learning (the acquisition of information and rules for using the information), reasoning (using rules to reach approximate or definite conclusions) and self-correction. Particular applications of AI include expert systems, speech recognition and machine vision.

Artificial Intelligence is the science and engineering of making intelligent machines, especially intelligent computer programs.

Artificial Intelligence is a way of making a computer, a computer-controlled robot, or a software think intelligently, in a similar manner the intelligent humans think.

Artificial Intelligence is accomplished by studying how human brain thinks, and how humans learn, decide, and work while trying to solve a problem, and then using the outcomes of this study as a basis of developing intelligent software and systems.

Artificial intelligence refers to the capability of certain techniques and tools which enables them to increase the knowledge initially provided to them through a process of inference or 'learning'. The so-called 'knowledge-based' or 'expert' systems are examples of artificial intelligence (AI). The essence of these systems is their ability to acquire heuristic knowledge, usually represented through a set of qualitative conditional expressions with verbal meaning, with the merit of being semantically clear. They are able to increase the initial knowledge base through a process of inference or 'learning'. Due to this, AI systems can be 'trained' to recognise patterns or signals and to respond to them.

On the other hand, Artificial intelligence (AI) is the discipline of computer perception, reasoning, and action. Dealing with uncertainty is a central challenge for artificial intelligence. Uncertainty management capabilities are required to combine evidence about a new situation with knowledge about similar situations, to draw inferences, and predict the effects of actions. Numerical computing has traditionally focused on problems where measurement imprecision is the sole source of reasoning uncertainty. AI researchers aim to develop software systems for applications such as automated learning, perception, natural language, and speech understanding. Such systems must deal with many sources of uncertainty: including equally plausible alternative explanations; missing information; incorrect object and event typing; diffuse evidence; ambiguous references; prediction of future events; and deliberate deception

History

Thought-capable artificial beings appeared as storytelling devices in antiquity, and have been common in fiction, as in Mary Shelley's Frankenstein or Karel Čapek's R.U.R. (Rossum's Universal Robots). These characters and their fates raised many of the same issues now discussed in the ethics of artificial intelligence.

The study of mechanical or "formal" reasoning began with philosophers and mathematicians in antiquity. The study of mathematical logic led directly to Alan Turing's theory of computation, which suggested that a machine, by shuffling symbols as simple as "0" and "1", could simulate any conceivable act of mathematical deduction. This insight, that digital computers can simulate any process of formal reasoning, is known as the Church–Turing thesis. Along with concurrent discoveries in neurobiology, information theory and cybernetics, this led researchers to consider the possibility of building an electronic brain. Turing proposed changing the question from whether a machine was intelligent, to "whether or not it is possible for machinery to show intelligent behaviour". The first work that is now generally recognized as AI was McCullouch and Pitts' 1943 formal design for Turing-complete "artificial neurons".

The field of AI research was born at a workshop at Dartmouth College in 1956, where the term "Artificial Intelligence" was coined by John McCarthy to distinguish the field from cybernetics and escape the influence of the cyberneticist Norbert Wiener. Attendees Allen Newell (CMU), Herbert Simon (CMU), John McCarthy (MIT), Marvin Minsky (MIT) and Arthur Samuel (IBM) became the founders and leaders of AI research. They and their students produced programs that the press described as "astonishing": computers were learning checkers strategies (c. 1954) (and by 1959 were reportedly playing better than the average human), solving word problems in algebra, proving logical theorems (Logic Theorist, first-run c. 1956) and speaking English. By the middle of the 1960s, research in the U.S. was heavily funded by the Department of Defense and laboratories had been established around the world. AI's founders were optimistic about the future: Herbert Simon predicted, "machines will be capable, within twenty years, of doing any work a man can do". Marvin Minsky agreed, writing, "within a generation ... the problem of creating 'artificial intelligence' will substantially be solved".

They failed to recognize the difficulty of some of the remaining tasks. Progress slowed and in 1974, in response to the criticism of Sir James Lighthill and ongoing pressure from the US Congress to fund more productive projects, both the U.S. and British governments cut off exploratory research in AI.

The next few years would later be called an "AI winter", a period when obtaining funding for AI projects was difficult.

In the early 1980s, AI research was revived by the commercial success of expert systems, a form of AI program that simulated the knowledge and analytical skills of human experts. By 1985, the market for AI had reached over a billion dollars. At the same time, Japan's fifth-generation computer project inspired the U.S and British governments to restore funding for academic research. However, beginning with the collapse of the Lisp Machine market in 1987, AI once again fell into disrepute, and a second, longer-lasting hiatus began.

In the late 1990s and early 21st century, AI began to be used for logistics, data mining, medical diagnosis and other areas. The success was due to increasing computational power (see Moore's law), greater emphasis on solving specific problems, new ties between AI and other fields (such as statistics, economics and mathematics), and a commitment by researchers to mathematical methods and scientific standards. Deep Blue became the first computer chess-playing system to beat a reigning world chess champion, Garry Kasparov, on 11 May 1997.

In 2011, a Jeopardy! quiz show exhibition match, IBM's question answering system, Watson, defeated the two greatest Jeopardy! champions, Brad Rutter and Ken Jennings, by a significant margin. Faster computers, algorithmic improvements, and access to large amounts of data enabled advances in machine learning and perception; data-hungry deep learning methods started to dominate accuracy benchmarks around 2012. The Kinect, which provides a 3D body–motion interface for the Xbox 360 and the Xbox One, uses algorithms that emerged from lengthy AI research as do intelligent personal assistants in smartphones. In March 2016, AlphaGo won 4 out of 5 games of Go in a match with Go champion Lee Sedol, becoming the first computer Go-playing system to beat a professional Go player without handicaps. In the 2017 Future of Go Summit, AlphaGo won a three-game match with Ke Jie, who at the time continuously held the world No. 1 ranking for two years. This marked the completion of a significant milestone in the development of Artificial Intelligence as Go is a relatively complex game, more so than Chess.

According to Bloomberg's Jack Clark, 2015 was a landmark year for artificial intelligence, with the number of software projects that use AI Google increased from a "sporadic usage" in 2012 to more than 2,700 projects. Clark also presents factual data indicating the improvements of AI since 2012 supported by lower error rates in image processing tasks. He attributes this to an increase in affordable neural networks, due to a rise in cloud computing infrastructure and to an increase in research tools and datasets. Other cited examples include Microsoft's development of a Skype system that can automatically translate from one language to another and Facebook's system that can describe images to blind people. In a 2017 survey, one in five companies reported they had "incorporated AI in some offerings or processes". Around 2016, China greatly accelerated its government funding; given its large supply of data and its rapidly increasing research output, some observers believe it may be on track to becoming an "AI superpower". However, it has been acknowledged that reports regarding artificial intelligence have tended to be exaggerated

Basics

A typical AI analyzes its environment and takes actions that maximize its chance of success. An AI's intended utility function (or goal) can be simple ("1 if the AI wins a game of Go, 0 otherwise") or complex ("Do mathematically similar actions to the ones succeeded in the past"). Goals can be explicitly defined or induced. If the AI is programmed for "reinforcement learning", goals can be implicitly induced by rewarding some types of behaviour or punishing others.[a]

Alternatively, an evolutionary system can induce goals by using a "fitness function" to mutate and preferentially replicate high-scoring AI systems, similarly to how animals evolved to innately desire certain goals such as finding food. Some AI systems, such as nearest-neighbour, instead of reason by analogy, these systems are not generally given goals, except to the degree that goals are implicit in their training data. Such systems can still be benchmarked if the non-goal system is framed as a system whose "goal" is to successfully accomplish its narrow classification task.

AI often revolves around the use of algorithms. An algorithm is a set of unambiguous instructions that a mechanical computer can execute.[b] A complex algorithm is often built on top of other, simpler, algorithms. A simple example of an algorithm is the following (optimal for the first player) recipe for play at tic-tac-toe:

If someone has a "threat" (that is, two in a row), take the remaining square. Otherwise, if a move "forks" to create two threats at once, play that move. Otherwise, take the center square if it is free. Otherwise, if your opponent has played in a corner, take the opposite corner. Otherwise, take an empty corner if one exists. Otherwise, take any empty square.

Many AI algorithms are capable of learning from data; they can enhance themselves by learning new heuristics (strategies, or "rules of thumb", that have worked well in the past), or can themselves write other algorithms. Some of the "learners" described below, including Bayesian networks, decision trees, and nearest-neighbour, could theoretically, (given infinite data, time, and memory) learn to approximate any function, including which combination of mathematical functions would best describe the world[citation needed]. These learners could therefore, derive all possible knowledge, by considering every possible hypothesis and matching them against the data. In practice, it is almost never possible to consider every possibility, because of the phenomenon of "combinatorial explosion", where the amount of time needed to solve a problem grows exponentially. Much of AI research involves figuring out how to identify and avoid considering a broad range of possibilities that are unlikely to be beneficial. For example, when viewing a map and looking for the shortest driving route from Denver to New York in the East, one can in most cases skip looking at any path through San Francisco or other areas far to the West; thus, an AI wielding a pathfinding algorithm like A* can avoid the combinatorial explosion that would ensue if every possible route had to be ponderously considered in turn.

The earliest (and easiest to understand) approach to AI was symbolism (such as formal logic): "If an otherwise healthy adult has a fever, then they may have influenza". A second, more general, approach is Bayesian inference: "If the current patient has a fever, adjust the probability they have influenza in a such-and-such way". The third major approach, extremely popular in routine business AI applications, are analogizers such as SVM and nearest-neighbour: "After examining the records of known past patients whose temperature, symptoms, age, and other factors mostly match the current patient, X% of those patients turned out to have influenza". A fourth approach is harder to intuitively understand, but is inspired by how the brain's machinery works: the artificial neural network approach uses artificial "neurons" that can learn by comparing itself to the desired output and altering the strengths of the connections between its internal neurons to "reinforce" connections that seemed to be useful. These four main approaches can overlap with each other and with evolutionary systems; for example, neural nets can learn to make inferences, to generalize, and to make analogies. Some systems implicitly or explicitly use multiple of these approaches, alongside many other AI and non-AI algorithms; the best approach is often different depending on the problem.

Learning algorithms work on the basis that strategies, algorithms, and inferences that worked well in the past are likely to continue working well in the future. These inferences can be obvious, such as "since the sun rose every morning for the last 10,000 days, it will probably rise tomorrow morning as well". They can be nuanced, such as "X% of families have geographically separate species with colour variants, so there is a Y% chance that undiscovered black swans exist". Learners also work on the basis of "Occam's razor": The simplest theory that explains the data is the likeliest. Therefore, according to Occam's razor principle, a learner must be designed such that it prefers simpler theories to complex theories, except in cases where the complex theory is proven substantially better.

Settling on a bad, overly complex theory gerrymandered to fit all the past training data is known as overfitting. Many systems attempt to reduce overfitting by rewarding a theory in accordance with how well it fits the data but penalizing the theory in accordance with how complex the theory is. Besides classic overfitting, learners can also disappoint by "learning the wrong lesson". A toy example is that an image classifier trained only on pictures of brown horses and black cats might conclude that all brown patches are likely to be horses. A real-world example is that, unlike humans, current image classifiers don't determine the spatial relationship between components of the picture; instead, they learn abstract patterns of pixels that humans are oblivious to, but that linearly correlate with images of certain types of real objects. Faintly superimposing such a pattern on legitimate image results in an "adversarial" image that the system misclassifies.

Compared with humans, existing AI lacks several features of human "commonsense reasoning"; most notably, humans have powerful mechanisms for reasoning about "naïve physics" such as space, time, and physical interactions. This enables even young children to easily make inferences like "If I roll this pen off a table, it will fall on the floor". Humans also have a powerful mechanism of "folk psychology" that helps them to interpret natural-language sentences such as "The city councilmen refused the demonstrators a permit because they advocated violence". (A generic AI has difficulty discerning whether the ones alleged to be advocating violence are the councilmen or the demonstrators.) This lack of "common knowledge" means that AI often makes different mistakes than humans make, in ways that can seem incomprehensible. For example, existing self-driving cars cannot reason about the location nor the intentions of pedestrians in the exact way that humans do and instead must use non-human modes of reasoning to avoid accidents.

Challenges of AI

The cognitive capabilities of current architectures are very limited, using only a simplified version of what intelligence is really capable of. For instance, the human mind has come up with ways to reason beyond measure and logical explanations to different occurrences in life. What would have been otherwise straightforward, an equivalently difficult problem may be challenging to solve computationally as opposed to using the human mind. This gives rise to two classes of models: structuralist and functionalist. The structural models aim to loosely mimic the basic intelligence operations of the mind such as reasoning and logic. The functional model refers to the correlating data to its computed counterpart.

The overall research goal of artificial intelligence is to create technology that allows computers and machines to function in an intelligent manner. The general problem of simulating (or creating) intelligence has been broken down into sub-problems. These consist of particular traits or capabilities that researchers expect an intelligent system to display. The traits described below have received the most attention.

Reasoning, problem-solving

Early researchers developed algorithms that imitated step-by-step reasoning that humans use when they solve puzzles or make logical deductions. By the late 1980s and 1990s, AI research had developed methods for dealing with uncertain or incomplete information, employing concepts from probability and economics.

These algorithms proved to be insufficient for solving large reasoning problems because they experienced a "combinatorial explosion": they became exponentially slower as the problems grew larger. In fact, even humans rarely use the step-by-step deduction that early AI research was able to model. They solve most of their problems using fast, intuitive judgements.

Knowledge representation

Knowledge representation and knowledge engineering are central to classical AI research. Some "expert systems" attempt to gather together explicit knowledge possessed by experts in some narrow domain. In addition, some projects attempt to gather the "commonsense knowledge" known to the average person into a database containing extensive knowledge about the world. Among the things a comprehensive commonsense knowledge base would contain are: objects, properties, categories and relations between objects; situations, events, states and time;[88] causes and effects; knowledge about knowledge (what we know about what other people know); and many other, less well-researched domains. A representation of "what exists" is an ontology: the set of objects, relations, concepts, and properties formally described so that software agents can interpret them. The semantics of these are captured as description logic concepts, roles, and individuals, and typically implemented as classes, properties, and individuals in the Web Ontology Language. The most general ontologies are called upper ontologies, which attempt to provide a foundation for all other knowledge by acting as mediators between domain ontologies that cover specific knowledge about a particular knowledge domain (field of interest or area of concern). Such formal knowledge representations can be used in content-based indexing and retrieval, scene interpretation, clinical decision support, knowledge discovery (mining "interesting" and actionable inferences from large databases), and other areas.

Among the most difficult problems in knowledge representation are:

Default ireasoning iand ithe iqualification iproblem

Many of the things people know take the form of "working assumptions". For example, if a bird comes up in conversation, people typically picture an animal that is fist-sized, sings, and flies. None of these things are true about all birds. John McCarthy identified this problem in 1969 as the qualification problem: for any commonsense rule that AI researchers care to represent, there tend to be a huge number of exceptions. Almost nothing is simply true or false in the way that abstract logic requires. AI research has explored a number of solutions to this problem.

The breadth of commonsense knowledge

The number of atomic facts that the average person knows is very large. Research projects that attempt to build a complete knowledge base of commonsense knowledge (e.g., Cyc) require enormous amounts of laborious ontological engineering they must be built, by hand, one complicated concept at a time.

The subsymbolic form of some commonsense knowledge

Much of what people know is not represented as "facts" or "statements" that they could express verbally. For example, a chess master will avoid a particular chess position because it "feels too exposed" or an art critic can take one look at a statue and realize that it is a fake. These are non-conscious and sub-symbolic intuitions or tendencies in the human brain.

Knowledge like this informs, supports and provides a context for symbolic, conscious knowledge. As with the related problem of sub-symbolic reasoning, it is hoped that situated AI, computational intelligence, or statistical AI will provide ways to represent this kind of knowledge.

Planning

Intelligent agents must be able to set goals and achieve them. They need a way to visualize the future—a representation of the state of the world and be able to make predictions about how their actions will change it—and be able to make choices that maximize the utility (or "value") of available choices.

In classical planning problems, the agent can assume that it is the only system acting in the world, allowing the agent to be certain of the consequences of its actions. However, if the agent is not the only actor, then it requires that the agent can reason under uncertainty. This calls for an agent that can not only assess its environment and make predictions but also evaluate, its predictions and adapt based on its assessment.

Multi-agent planning uses the cooperation and competition of many agents to achieve a given goal. Emergent behaviour such as this is used by evolutionary algorithms and swarm intelligence.

Learning

Machine learning (ML), a fundamental concept of AI research since the field's inception, is the study of computer algorithms that improve automatically through experience.

Unsupervised learning is the ability to find patterns in a stream of input, without requiring a human to label the inputs first. Supervised learning includes both classification and numerical regression, which requires a human to label the input data first. Classification is used to determine what category something belongs in, and occurs after a program sees a number of examples of things from several categories.

Regression is the attempt to produce a function that describes the relationship between inputs and outputs and predicts how the outputs should change as the inputs change. Both classifiers and regression learners can be viewed as "function approximators" trying to learn an unknown (possibly implicit) function; for example, a spam classifier can be viewed as learning a function that maps from the text of an email to one of two categories, "spam" or "not spam". Computational learning theory can assess learners by computational complexity, by sample complexity (how much data is required), or by other notions of optimization. In reinforcement learning the agent is rewarded for good responses and punished for bad ones. The agent uses this sequence of rewards and punishments to form a strategy for operating in its problem space.

Natural language processing

Natural language processing (NLP) gives machines the ability to read and understand human language. A sufficiently powerful natural language processing system would enable natural-language user interfaces and the acquisition of knowledge directly from human-written sources, such as newswire texts. Some straightforward applications of natural language processing include information retrieval, text mining, question answering and machine translation. Many current approaches use word co-occurrence frequencies to construct syntactic representations of text. "Keyword spotting" strategies for search are popular and scalable but dumb; a search query for "dog" might only match documents with the literal word "dog" and miss a document with the word "poodle". "Lexical affinity" strategies use the occurrence of words such as "accident" to assess the sentiment of a document. Modern statistical NLP approaches can combine all these strategies as well as others, and often achieve acceptable accuracy at the page or paragraph level, but continue to lack the semantic understanding required to classify isolated sentences well. Besides the usual difficulties with encoding semantic commonsense knowledge, existing semantic NLP sometimes scales too poorly to be viable in business applications. Beyond semantic NLP, the ultimate goal of "narrative" NLP is to embody a full understanding of commonsense reasoning.

Perception

Machine perception is the ability to use input from sensors (such as cameras (visible spectrum or infrared), microphones, wireless signals, and active lidar, sonar, radar, and tactile sensors) to deduce aspects of the world. Applications include speech recognition, facial recognition, and object recognition. Computer vision is the ability to analyze visual input. Such input is usually ambiguous; a giant, fifty-meter-tall pedestrian far away may produce exactly the same pixels as a nearby normal-sized pedestrian, requiring the AI to judge the relative likelihood and reasonableness of different interpretations, for example by using its "object model" to assess that fifty-meter pedestrians do not exist.

Motion and manipulation

AI is heavily used in robotics. Advanced robotic arms and other industrial robots, widely used in modern factories, can learn from experience how to move efficiently despite the presence of friction and gear slippage. A modern mobile robot, when given a small, static, and visible environment, can easily determine its location and map its environment; however, dynamic environments, such as (in endoscopy) the interior of a patient's breathing body, pose a greater challenge. Motion planning is the process of breaking down a movement task into "primitives" such as individual joint movements. Such movement often involves compliant motion, a process where movement requires maintaining physical contact with an object. Moravec's paradox generalizes that low-level sensorimotor skills that humans take for granted are, counterintuitively, difficult to program into a robot; the paradox is named after Hans Moravec, who stated in 1988 that "it is comparatively easy to make computers exhibit adult level performance on intelligence tests or playing checkers, and difficult or impossible to give them the skills of a one-year-old when it comes to perception and mobility". This is attributed to the fact that, unlike checkers, physical dexterity has been a direct target of natural selection for millions of years.

Social intelligence

Moravec's paradox can be extended to many forms of social intelligence. Distributed multi-agent coordination of autonomous vehicles remains a difficult problem. Affective computing is an interdisciplinary umbrella that comprises systems which recognize, interpret, process, or simulate human effects. Moderate successes related to affective computing include textual sentiment analysis and, more recently, multimodal affect analysis (see multimodal sentiment analysis), wherein AI classifies the effects displayed by a videotaped subject.

In the long run, social skills and an understanding of human emotion and game theory would be valuable to a social agent. Being able to predict the actions of others by understanding their motives and emotional states would allow an agent to make better decisions. Some computer systems mimic human emotion and expressions to appear more sensitive to the emotional dynamics of human interaction, or to otherwise facilitate human-computer interaction. Similarly, some virtual assistants are programmed to speak conversationally or even to banter humorously; this tends to give naïve users an unrealistic conception of how intelligent existing computer agents actually are.

General intelligence

Historically, projects such as the Cyc knowledge base (1984–) and the massive Japanese Fifth Generation Computer Systems initiative (1982–1992) attempted to cover the breadth of human cognition. These early projects failed to escape the limitations of non-quantitative symbolic logic models and, in retrospect, greatly underestimated the difficulty of cross-domain AI. Nowadays, the vast majority of current AI researchers work instead on tractable "narrow AI" applications (such as medical diagnosis or automobile navigation). Many researchers predict that such "narrow AI" work in different individual domains will eventually be incorporated into a machine with artificial general intelligence (AGI), combining most of the narrow skills mentioned in this article and at some point even exceeding human ability in most or all these areas. Many advances have general, cross-domain significance. One high-profile example is that DeepMind in the 2010s developed a "generalized artificial intelligence" that could learn many diverse Atari games on its own, and later developed a variant of the system which succeeds at sequential learning. Besides transfer learning, hypothetical AGI breakthroughs could include the development of reflective architectures that can engage in decision-theoretic metareasoning, and figuring out how to "slurp up" a comprehensive knowledge base from the entire unstructured Web. Some argue that some kind of (currently-undiscovered) conceptually straightforward, but mathematically difficult, "Master Algorithm" could lead to AGI. Finally, a few "emergent" approaches look to simulating human intelligence extremely closely, and believe that anthropomorphic features like an artificial brain or simulated child development may someday reach a critical point where general intelligence emerges.

Many of the problems in this article may also require general intelligence, if machines are to solve the problems as well as people do. For example, even specific straightforward tasks, like machine translation, require that a machine read and write in both languages (NLP), follow the author's argument (reason), know what is being talked about (knowledge), and faithfully reproduce the author's original intent (social intelligence). A problem like machine translation is considered "AI-complete", because all of these problems need to be solved simultaneously in order to reach human-level machine performance.

Approaches

There is no established unifying theory or paradigm that guides AI research. Researchers disagree about many issues. A few of the most long-standing questions that have remained unanswered are these: should artificial intelligence simulate natural intelligence by studying psychology or neurobiology? Or is human biology as irrelevant to AI research as bird biology is to aeronautical engineering? Can intelligent behaviour be described using simple, elegant principles (such as logic or optimization)? Or does it necessarily require solving a large number of completely unrelated problems?

Cybernetics and brain simulation

In the 1940s and 1950s, a number of researchers explored the connection between neurobiology, information theory, and cybernetics. Some of them built machines that used electronic networks to exhibit rudimentary intelligence, such as W. Grey Walter's turtles and the Johns Hopkins Beast. Many of these researchers gathered for meetings of the Teleological Society at Princeton University and the Ratio Club in England. By 1960, this approach was largely abandoned, although elements of it would be revived in the 1980s.

Symbolic

When access to digital computers became possible in the mid-1950s, AI research began to explore the possibility that human intelligence could be reduced to symbol manipulation. The research was centered in three institutions: Carnegie Mellon University, Stanford and MIT, and as described below, each one developed its own style of research. John Haugeland named these symbolic approaches to AI "good old fashioned AI" or "GOFAI". During the 1960s, symbolic approaches had achieved great success at simulating high-level "thinking" in small demonstration programs. Approaches based on cybernetics or artificial neural networks were abandoned or pushed into the background. Researchers in the 1960s and the 1970s were convinced that symbolic approaches would eventually succeed in creating a machine with artificial general intelligence and considered this the goal of their field.

Cognitive simulation

Economist Herbert Simon and Allen Newell studied human problem-solving skills and attempted to formalize them, and their work laid the foundations of the field of artificial intelligence, as well as cognitive science, operations research and management science. Their research team used the results of psychological experiments to develop programs that simulated the techniques that people used to solve problems. This tradition, centered at Carnegie Mellon University would eventually culminate in the development of the Soar architecture in the middle 1980s.

Logic-based

Unlike Simon and Newell, John McCarthy felt that machines did not need to simulate human thought, but should instead try to find the essence of abstract reasoning and problem-solving, regardless whether people used the same algorithms. His laboratory at Stanford (SAIL) focused on using formal logic to solve a wide variety of problems, including knowledge representation, planning and learning. Logic was also the focus of the work at the University of Edinburgh and elsewhere in Europe which led to the development of the programming language Prolog and the science of logic programming.

Anti-logic or scruffy

Researchers at MIT (such as Marvin Minsky and Seymour Papert) found that solving difficult problems in vision and natural language processing required ad-hoc solutions—they argued that there was no simple and general principle (like logic) that would capture all the aspects of intelligent behaviour. Roger Schank described their "anti-logic" approaches as "scruffy" (as opposed to the "neat" paradigms at CMU and Stanford). Commonsense knowledge bases (such as Doug Lenat's Cyc) are an example of "scruffy" AI, since they must be built by hand, one complicated concept at a time.

Knowledge-based

When computers with large memories became available around 1970, researchers from all three traditions began to build knowledge into AI applications. This "knowledge revolution" led to the development and deployment of expert systems (introduced by Edward Feigenbaum), the first truly successful form of AI software. A key component of the system architecture for all expert systems is the knowledge base, which stores facts and rules that illustrate AI. The knowledge revolution was also driven by the realization that enormous amounts of knowledge would be required by many simple AI applications.

Sub-symbolic

By the 1980s, progress in symbolic AI seemed to stall and many believed that symbolic systems would never be able to imitate all the processes of human cognition, especially perception, robotics, learning and pattern recognition. A number of researchers began to look into "sub-symbolic" approaches to specific AI problems. Sub-symbolic methods manage to approach intelligence without specific representations of knowledge.

Embodied intelligence

This includes embodied, situated, behaviour-based, and nouvelle AI. Researchers from the related field of robotics, such as Rodney Brooks, rejected symbolic AI and focused on the basic engineering problems that would allow robots to move and survive. Their work revived the non-symbolic point of view of the early cybernetics researchers of the 1950s and reintroduced the use of control theory in AI. This coincided with the development of the embodied mind thesis in the related field of cognitive science: the idea that aspects of the body (such as movement, perception and visualization) are required for higher intelligence.

Within developmental robotics, developmental learning approaches are elaborated upon to allow robots to accumulate repertoires of novel skills through autonomous self-exploration, social interaction with human teachers, and the use of guidance mechanisms (active learning, maturation, motor synergies, etc.).

Computational intelligence and soft computing

Interest in neural networks and "connectionism" was revived by David Rumelhart and others in the middle of the 1980s. Artificial neural networks are an example of soft computing—they are solutions to problems which cannot be solved with complete logical certainty, and where an approximate solution is often sufficient. Other soft computing approaches to AI include fuzzy systems, Grey system theory, evolutionary computation and many statistical tools. The application of soft computing to AI is studied collectively by the emerging discipline of computational intelligence.

Statistical learning

Much of traditional GOFAI got bogged down on ad hoc patches to symbolic computation that worked on their own toy models but failed to generalize to real-world results. However, around the 1990s, AI researchers adopted sophisticated mathematical tools, such as hidden Markov models (HMM), information theory, and normative Bayesian decision theory to compare or to unify competing architectures. The shared mathematical language permitted a high level of collaboration with more established fields (like mathematics, economics or operations research). Compared with GOFAI, new "statistical learning" techniques such as HMM and neural networks were gaining higher levels of accuracy in many practical domains such as data mining, without necessarily acquiring a semantic understanding of the datasets. The increased successes with real-world data led to increasing emphasis on comparing different approaches against shared test data to see which approach performed best in a broader context than that provided by idiosyncratic toy models; AI research was becoming more scientific. Nowadays results of experiments are often rigorously measurable, and are sometimes (with difficulty) reproducible. Different statistical learning techniques have different limitations; for example, basic HMM cannot model the infinite possible combinations of natural language. Critics note that the shift from GOFAI to statistical learning is often also a shift away from explainable AI. In AGI research, some scholars caution against over-reliance on statistical learning, and argue that continuing research into GOFAI will still be necessary to attain general intelligence.

Integrating the approaches

- ### Intelligent agent paradigm

An intelligent agent is a system that perceives its environment and takes actions which maximize its chances of success. The simplest intelligent agents are programs that solve specific problems. More complicated agents include human beings and organizations of human beings (such as firms). The paradigm allows researchers to directly compare or even combine different approaches to isolated problems, by asking which agent is best at maximizing a given "goal function". An agent that solves a specific problem can use any approach that works—some agents are symbolic and logical, some are sub-symbolic artificial neural networks and others may use new approaches. The paradigm also gives researchers a common language to communicate with other fields—such as decision theory and economics—that also use concepts of abstract agents. Building a complete agent requires researchers to address realistic problems of integration; for example, because sensory systems give uncertain information about the environment, planning systems must be able to function in the presence of uncertainty. The intelligent agent paradigm became widely accepted during the 1990s.

- **Agent architectures and cognitive architectures**

Researchers have designed systems to build intelligent systems out of interacting intelligent agents in a multi-agent system. A hierarchical control system provides a bridge between sub-symbolic AI at its lowest, reactive levels and traditional symbolic AI at its highest levels, where relaxed time constraints permit planning and world modelling. Some cognitive architectures are custom-built to solve a narrow problem; others, such as Soar, are designed to mimic human cognition and to provide insight into general intelligence. Modern extensions of Soar are hybrid intelligent systems that include both symbolic and sub-symbolic components.

Tools

Artificial intelligence has developed many tools to solve the most difficult problems in computer science. A few of the most general of these methods are discussed below.

Search and optimization

Many problems in Artificial intelligence can be solved in theory by intelligently searching through many possible solutions: Reasoning can be reduced to performing a search. For example, logical proof can be viewed as searching for a path that leads from premises to conclusions, where each step is the application of an inference rule. Planning algorithms search through trees of goals and subgoals, attempting to find a path to a target goal, a process called means-ends analysis. Robotics algorithms for moving limbs and grasping objects use local searches in configuration space. Many learning algorithms use search algorithms based on optimization.

Simple exhaustive searches are rarely sufficient for most real-world problems: the search space (the number of places to search) quickly grows to astronomical numbers. The result is a search that is too slow or never completes. The solution, for many problems, is to use "heuristics" or "rules of thumb" that prioritize choices in favour of those that are more likely to reach a goal and to do so in a shorter number of steps. In some search methodologies heuristics can also serve to entirely eliminate some choices that are unlikely to lead to a goal (called "pruning the search tree"). Heuristics supply the program with a "best guess" for the path on which the solution lies. Heuristics limit the search for solutions into a smaller sample size.

A very different kind of search came to prominence in the 1990s, based on the mathematical theory of optimization. For many problems, it is possible to begin the search with some form of a guess and then refine the guess incrementally until no more refinements can be made. These algorithms can be visualized as blind hill climbing: we begin the search at a random point on the landscape, and then, by jumps or steps, we keep moving our guess uphill, until we reach the top. Other optimization algorithms are simulated annealing, beam search and random optimization.

Evolutionary computation uses a form of optimization search. For example, they may begin with a population of organisms (the guesses) and then allow them to mutate and recombine, selecting only the fittest to survive each generation (refining the guesses). Classic evolutionary algorithms include genetic algorithms, gene expression programming, and genetic programming. Alternatively, distributed search processes can coordinate via swarm intelligence algorithms. Two popular swarm algorithms used in search are particle swarm optimization (inspired by bird flocking) and ant colony optimization (inspired by ant trails).

Logic

Logic is used for knowledge representation and problem-solving, but it can be applied to other problems as well. For example, the satplan algorithm uses logic for planning and inductive logic programming is a method for learning.

Several different forms of logic are used in AI research. Propositional logic involves truth functions such as "or" and "not". First-order logic adds quantifiers and predicates, and can express facts about objects, their properties, and their relations with each other. Fuzzy set theory assigns a "degree of truth" (between 0 and 1) to vague statements such as "Alice is old" (or rich, or tall, or hungry) that are too linguistically imprecise to be completely true or false. Fuzzy logic is successfully used in control systems to allow experts to contribute vague rules such as "if you are close to the destination station and moving fast, increase the train's brake pressure"; these vague rules can then be numerically refined within the system. Fuzzy logic fails to scale well in knowledge bases; many Artificial intelligence researchers question the validity of chaining fuzzy-logic inferences.

Default logics, non-monotonic logics and circumscription are forms of logic designed to help with default reasoning and the qualification problem. Several extensions of logic have been designed to handle specific domains of knowledge, such as: description logics; situation calculus, event calculus and fluent calculus (for representing events and time);[88] causal calculus; belief calculus; and modal logics.

Overall, qualitative symbolic logic is brittle and scales poorly in the presence of noise or other uncertainty. Exceptions to rules are numerous, and it is difficult for logical systems to function in the presence of contradictory rules.

Probabilistic methods for uncertain reasoning

Many problems in Artificial intelligence (in reasoning, planning, learning, perception, and robotics) require the agent to operate with incomplete or uncertain information. AI researchers have devised a number of powerful tools to solve these problems using methods from probability theory and economics.

Bayesian networks are a very general tool that can be used for various problems: reasoning (using the Bayesian inference algorithm), learning (using the expectation-maximization algorithm), planning (using decision networks) and perception (using dynamic Bayesian networks). Probabilistic algorithms can also be used for filtering, prediction, smoothing and finding explanations for streams of data, helping perception systems to analyze processes that occur over time (e.g., hidden Markov models or Kalman filters). Compared with symbolic logic, formal Bayesian inference is computationally expensive. For inference to be tractable, most observations must be conditionally independent of one another. Complicated graphs with diamonds or other "loops" (undirected cycles) can require a sophisticated method such as Markov chain Monte Carlo, which spreads an ensemble of random walkers throughout the Bayesian network and attempts to converge to an assessment of the conditional probabilities. Bayesian networks are used on Xbox Live to rate and match players; wins and losses are "evidence" of how good a player is[citation needed]. AdSense uses a Bayesian network with over 300 million edges to learn which ads to serve.

A key concept from the science of economics is "utility": a measure of how valuable something is to an intelligent agent. Precise mathematical tools have been developed that analyze how an agent can make choices and plan, using decision theory, decision analysis, and information value theory. These tools include models such as Markov decision processes, dynamic decision networks, game theory and mechanism design.

Classifiers and statistical learning methods

The simplest AI applications can be divided into two types: classifiers ("if shiny then diamond") and controllers ("if shiny then pick up"). Controllers do, however, also classify conditions before inferring actions, and therefore classification forms a central part of many AI systems. Classifiers are functions that use pattern matching to determine a closest match. They can be tuned according to examples, making them very attractive for use in Artificial intelligence. These examples are known as observations or patterns. In supervised learning, each pattern belongs to a certain predefined class. A class can be seen as a decision that has to be made. All the observations combined with their class labels are known as a data set. When a new observation is received, that observation is classified based on previous experience.

A classifier can be trained in various ways; there are many statistical and machine learning approaches. The decision tree is perhaps the most widely used machine learning algorithm. Other widely used classifiers are the neural network, k-nearest neighbour algorithm, kernel methods such as the support vector machine (SVM), Gaussian mixture model, and the extremely popular naive Bayes classifier. Classifier performance depends greatly on the characteristics of the data to be classified, such as the dataset size, distribution of samples across classes, the dimensionality, and the level of noise. Model-based classifiers perform well if the assumed model is an extremely good fit for the actual data. Otherwise, if no matching model is available, and if accuracy (rather than speed or scalability) is the sole concern, conventional wisdom is that discriminative classifiers (especially SVM) tend to be more accurate than model-based classifiers such as "naive Bayes" on most practical data sets.

Artificial neural networks

Neural networks were inspired by the architecture of neurons in the human brain. A simple "neuron" N accepts input from other neurons, each of which, when activated (or "fired"), cast a weighted "vote" for or against whether neuron N should itself activate. Learning requires an algorithm to adjust these weights based on the training data; one simple algorithm (dubbed "fire together, wire together") is to increase the weight between two connected neurons when the activation of one triggers the successful activation of another. The neural network forms "concepts" that are distributed among a subnetwork of shared neurons that tend to fire together; a concept meaning "leg" might be coupled with a subnetwork meaning "foot" that includes the sound for "foot". Neurons have a continuous spectrum of activation; in addition, neurons can process inputs in a nonlinear way rather than weighing straightforward votes. Modern neural networks can learn both continuous functions and, surprisingly, digital logical operations. Neural networks' early successes included predicting the stock market and (in 1995) a mostly self-driving car. In the 2010s, advances in neural networks using deep learning thrust AI into widespread public consciousness and contributed to an enormous upshift in corporate AI spending; for example, AI-related M&A in 2017 was over 25 times as large as in 2015.

The study of non-learning artificial neural networks began in the decade before the field of AI research was founded, in the work of Walter Pitts and Warren McCullouch. Frank Rosenblatt invented the perceptron, a learning network with a single layer, similar to the old concept of linear regression. Early pioneers also include Alexey Grigorevich Ivakhnenko, Teuvo Kohonen, Stephen Grossberg, Kunihiko Fukushima, Christoph von der Malsburg, David Willshaw, Shun-Ichi Amari, Bernard Widrow, John Hopfield, Eduardo R. Caianiello, and others[citation needed].

The main categories of networks are acyclic or feedforward neural networks (where the signal passes in only one direction) and recurrent neural networks (which allow feedback and short-term memories of previous input events). Among the most popular feedforward networks are perceptrons, multi-layer perceptrons and radial basis networks. Neural networks can be applied to the problem of intelligent control (for robotics) or learning, using such techniques as Hebbian learning ("fire together, wire together"), GMDH or competitive learning.

Today, neural networks are often trained by the backpropagation algorithm, which had been around since 1970 as the reverse mode of automatic differentiation published by Seppo Linnainmaa, and was introduced to neural networks by Paul Werbos.

Hierarchical temporal memory is an approach that models some of the structural and algorithmic properties of the neocortex.

To summarize, most neural networks use some form of gradient descent on a hand-created neural topology. However, some research groups, such as Uber, argue that simple neuroevolution to mutate new neural network topologies and weights may be competitive with sophisticated gradient descent approaches[citation needed]. One advantage of neuroevolution is that it may be less prone to get caught in "dead ends".

Deep feedforward neural networks

Deep learning is any artificial neural network that can learn a long chain of causal links[dubious – discuss]. For example, a feedforward network with six hidden layers can learn a seven-link causal chain (six hidden layers + output layer) and has a "credit assignment path" (CAP) depth of seven[citation needed]. Many deep learning systems need to be able to learn chains ten or more causal links in length. Deep learning has transformed many important subfields of artificial intelligence[why?], including computer vision, speech recognition, natural language processing and others.

According to one overview, the expression "Deep Learning" was introduced to the machine learning community by Rina Dechter in 1986 and gained traction after Igor Aizenberg and colleagues introduced it to artificial neural networks in 2000. The first functional Deep Learning networks were published by Alexey Grigorevich Ivakhnenko and V. G. Lapa in 1965. These networks are trained one layer at a time. Ivakhnenko's 1971 paper describes the learning of a deep feedforward multilayer perceptron with eight layers, already much deeper than many later networks. In 2006, a publication by Geoffrey Hinton and Ruslan Salakhutdinov introduced another way of pre-training many-layered feedforward neural networks (FNNs) one layer at a time, treating each layer in turn as an unsupervised restricted Boltzmann machine, then using supervised backpropagation for fine-tuning. Similar to shallow artificial neural networks, deep neural networks can model complex non-linear relationships. Over the last few years, advances in both machine learning algorithms and computer hardware have led to more efficient methods for training deep neural networks that contain many layers of non-linear hidden units and a very large output layer.

Deep learning often uses convolutional neural networks (CNNs), whose origins can be traced back to the Neocognitron introduced by Kunihiko Fukushima in 1980. In 1989, Yann LeCun and colleagues applied backpropagation to such an architecture. In the early 2000s, in an industrial application, CNNs already processed an estimated 10% to 20% of all the checks written in the US. Since 2011, fast implementations of CNNs on GPUs have won many visual pattern recognition competitions.

CNNs with 12 convolutional layers were used in conjunction with reinforcement learning by Deepmind's "AlphaGo Lee", the program that beat a top Go champion in 2016.

Deep recurrent neural networks

Early on, deep learning was also applied to sequence learning with recurrent neural networks (RNNs) which are in theory Turing complete and can run arbitrary programs to process arbitrary sequences of inputs. The depth of an RNN is unlimited and depends on the length of its input sequence; thus, an RNN is an example of deep learning. RNNs can be trained by gradient descent but suffer from the vanishing gradient problem. In 1992, it was shown that unsupervised pre-training of a stack of recurrent neural networks can speed up subsequent supervised learning of deep sequential problems.

Numerous researchers now use variants of a deep learning recurrent NN called the long short-term memory (LSTM) network published by Hochreiter & Schmidhuber in 1997. LSTM is often trained by Connectionist Temporal Classification (CTC). At Google, Microsoft and Baidu this approach has revolutionised speech recognition. For example, in 2015, Google's speech recognition experienced a dramatic performance jump of 49% through CTC-trained LSTM, which is now available through Google Voice to billions of smartphone users. Google also used LSTM to improve machine translation, Language Modeling and Multilingual Language Processing. LSTM combined with CNNs also improved automatic image captioning and a plethora of other applications.

Evaluating progress

AI, like electricity or the steam engine, is a general-purpose technology. There is no consensus on how to characterize which tasks AI tends to excel at. While projects such as AlphaZero have succeeded in generating their own knowledge from scratch, many other machine learning projects require large training datasets. Researcher Andrew Ng has suggested, as a "highly imperfect rule of thumb", that "almost anything a typical human can do with less than one second of mental thought, we can probably now or in the near future automate using AI."

Moravec's paradox suggests that AI lags humans at many tasks that the human brain has specifically evolved to perform well.

Games provide a well-publicized benchmark for assessing rates of progress. AlphaGo around 2016 brought the era of classical board-game benchmarks to a close. Games of imperfect knowledge provide new challenges to AI in the area of game theory. E-sports such as StarCraft continue to provide additional public benchmarks. There are many competitions and prizes, such as the Imagenet Challenge, to promote research in artificial intelligence. The most common areas of competition include general machine intelligence, conversational behaviour, data-mining, robotic cars, and robot soccer as well as conventional games.

The "imitation game" (an interpretation of the 1950 Turing test that assesses whether a computer can imitate a human) is nowadays considered too exploitable to be a meaningful benchmark. A derivative of the Turing test is the Completely Automated Public Turing test to tell Computers and Humans Apart (CAPTCHA). As the name implies, this helps to determine that a user is an actual person and not a computer posing as a human. In contrast to the standard Turing test, CAPTCHA is administered by a machine and targeted to a human as opposed to being administered by a human and targeted to a machine. A computer asks a user to complete a simple test then generates a grade for that test. Computers are unable to solve the problem, so correct solutions are deemed to be the result of a person taking the test. A common type of CAPTCHA is the test that requires the typing of distorted letters, numbers or symbols that appear in an image undecipherable by a computer.

Proposed "universal intelligence" tests aim to compare how well machines, humans, and even non-human animals perform on problem sets that are generic as possible. At an extreme, the test suite can contain every possible problem, weighted by

Kolmogorov complexity; unfortunately, these problem sets tend to be dominated by impoverished pattern-matching exercises where a tuned AI can easily exceed human performance levels.

Applications

Artificial intelligence is relevant to any intellectual task. Modern artificial intelligence techniques are pervasive and are too numerous to list here. Frequently, when a technique reaches mainstream use, it is no longer considered artificial intelligence; this phenomenon is described as the AI effect.

High-profile examples of Artificial intelligence include autonomous vehicles (such as drones and self-driving cars), medical diagnosis, creating art (such as poetry), proving mathematical theorems, playing games (such as Chess or Go), search engines (such as Google search), online assistants (such as Siri), image recognition in photographs, spam filtering, predicting flight delays, prediction of judicial decisions, targeting online advertisements, and energy storage

With social media sites overtaking TV as a source for news for young people and news organizations increasingly reliant on social media platforms for generating distribution, major publishers now use artificial intelligence (AI) technology to post stories more effectively and generate higher volumes of traffic.

Healthcare

Artificial intelligence in healthcare is often used for classification, whether to automate initial evaluation of a CT scan or EKG or to identify high-risk patients for population health. The breadth of applications is rapidly increasing. As an example, AI is being applied to the high-cost problem of dosage issues—where findings suggested that AI could save $16 billion. In 2016, a groundbreaking study in California found that a mathematical formula developed with the help of AI correctly determined the accurate dose of immunosuppressant drugs to give to organ patients.

Artificial intelligence is assisting doctors. According to Bloomberg Technology, Microsoft has developed AI to help doctors find the right treatments for cancer. There is a great amount of research and drugs developed relating to cancer. In detail, there are more than 800 medicines and vaccines to treat cancer. This negatively affects the doctors, because there are too many options to choose from, making it more difficult to choose the right drugs for the patients. Microsoft is working on a project to develop a machine called "Hanover"[citation needed]. Its goal is to memorize all the papers necessary to cancer and help predict which combinations of drugs will be most effective for each patient. One project that is being worked on at the moment is fighting myeloid leukemia, a fatal cancer where the treatment has not improved in decades. Another study was reported to have found that artificial intelligence was as good as trained doctors in identifying skin cancers. Another study is using artificial intelligence to try to monitor multiple high-risk patients, and this is done by asking each patient numerous questions based on data acquired from live doctor to patient interactions. One study was done with transfer learning, the machine performed a diagnosis similarly to a well-trained ophthalmologist, and could generate a decision within 30 seconds on whether or not the patient should be referred for treatment, with more than 95% accuracy.

According to CNN, a recent study by surgeons at the Children's National Medical Center in Washington successfully demonstrated surgery with an autonomous robot. The team supervised the robot while it performed soft-tissue surgery, stitching together a pig's bowel during open surgery, and doing so better than a human surgeon, the team claimed. IBM has created its own artificial intelligence computer, the IBM Watson, which has beaten human intelligence (at some levels). Watson has struggled to achieve success and adoption in healthcare.

Automotive

Advancements in AI have contributed to the growth of the automotive industry through the creation and evolution of self-driving vehicles. As of 2016, there are over 30 companies utilizing AI into the creation of driverless cars. A few companies involved with AI include Tesla, Google, and Apple.

Many components contribute to the functioning of self-driving cars. These vehicles incorporate systems such as braking, lane changing, collision prevention, navigation and mapping. Together, these systems, as well as high-performance computers, are integrated into one complex vehicle.

Recent developments in autonomous automobiles have made the innovation of self-driving trucks possible, though they are still in the testing phase. The UK government has passed legislation to begin testing of self-driving truck platoons in 2018. Self-driving truck platoons are a fleet of self-driving trucks following the lead of one non-self-driving truck, so the truck platoons aren't entirely autonomous yet. Meanwhile, the Daimler, a German automobile corporation, is testing the Freightliner Inspiration which is a semi-autonomous truck that will only be used on the highway.

One main factor that influences the ability for a driver-less automobile to function is mapping. In general, the vehicle would be pre-programmed with a map of the area being driven. This map would include data on the approximations of street light and curb heights in order for the vehicle to be aware of its surroundings. However, Google has been working on an algorithm with the purpose of eliminating the need for pre-programmed maps and instead, creating a device that would be able to adjust to a variety of new surroundings. Some self-driving cars are not equipped with steering wheels or brake pedals, so there has also been research focused on creating an algorithm that is capable of maintaining a safe environment for the passengers in the vehicle through awareness of speed and driving conditions.

Another factor that is influencing the ability of a driver-less automobile is the safety of the passenger. To make a driver-less automobile, engineers must program it to handle high-risk situations. These situations could include a head-on collision with pedestrians. The car's main goal should be to make a decision that would avoid hitting the pedestrians and saving the passengers in the car. But there is a possibility the car would need to make a decision that would put someone in danger. In other words, the car would need to decide to save the pedestrians or the passengers. The programming of the car in these situations is crucial to a successful driver-less automobile.

Finance and economics

Financial institutions have long used artificial neural network systems to detect charges or claims outside of the norm, flagging these for human investigation. The use of Artificial intelligence in banking can be traced back to 1987 when Security Pacific National Bank in the US set-up a Fraud Prevention Taskforce to counter the unauthorized use of debit cards.[299] Programs like Kasisto and Moneystream are using Artificial intelligence in financial services.

Banks use artificial intelligence systems today to organize operations, maintain book-keeping, invest in stocks, and manage properties. Artificial intelligence can react to changes overnight or when business is not taking place. In August 2001, robots beat humans in a simulated financial trading competition. Artificial intelligence has also reduced fraud and financial crimes by monitoring behavioural patterns of users for any abnormal changes or anomalies.

AI is also being used by corporations. Whereas Artificial intelligence CEO's are still 30 years away, robotic process automation (RPA) is already being used today in corporate finance. RPA uses artificial intelligence to train and teach software robots to process transactions, monitor compliance and audit processes automatically.

The use of Artificial intelligence machines in the market in applications such as online trading and decision making has changed major economic theories. For example, AI-based buying and selling platforms have changed the law of supply and demand in that it is now possible to easily estimate individualized demand and supply curves and thus individualized pricing. Furthermore, AI machines reduce information asymmetry in the market and thus making markets more efficient while reducing the volume of trades. Furthermore, Artificial intelligence in the markets limits the consequences of behaviour in the markets again making markets more efficient. Other theories where Artificial intelligence has had an impact include in rational choice, rational expectations, game theory, Lewis turning point, portfolio optimization and counterfactual thinking. In August 2019, the AICPA introduced AI training course for accounting professionals.

Government

Artificial intelligence paired with facial recognition systems may be used for mass surveillance. This is already the case in some parts of China. Artificial intelligence has also competed in the Tama City mayoral elections in 2018.

In 2019, the tech city of Bengaluru in India is set to deploy AI managed traffic signal systems across the 387 traffic signals in the city. This system will involve the use of cameras to ascertain traffic density and accordingly calculate the time needed to clear the traffic volume which will determine the signal duration for vehicular traffic across streets.

Higher education

Artificial intelligence is being implemented in university settings to aid in student learning, particularly for students with learning disabilities. With more students learning remotely and universities seeking ways to further provide assistive technologies to students who need it. These students include the 20,000 deaf or hard of hearing students who attend post-secondary educational institutions each year. AI is being used to capture important data, provide transcription and captioning live in lectures, and more. The Americans with Disabilities Act (ADA), which came into law in 1990, pushed many universities to invest more in assistive technologies which are rooted in Artificial intelligence. Now, universities are moving from a reactionary approach to this law which requires them to provide tools, but to implement Artificial intelligence technologies to aid in the learning of all students and create personalized learning experiences for them through video recommendations and more data.

Video games

In video games, artificial intelligence is routinely used to generate dynamic purposeful behaviour in non-player characters (NPCs). In addition, well-understood AI techniques are routinely used for pathfinding. Some researchers consider NPC AI in games to be a "solved problem" for most production tasks. Games with more atypical AI include the Artificial intelligence director of Left 4 Dead (2008) and the neuroevolutionary training of platoons in Supreme Commander 2 (2010).

Military

The main military applications of Artificial Intelligence and Machine Learning are to enhance C2, Communications, Sensors, Integration and Interoperability. Artificial Intelligence technologies enable coordination of sensors and effectors, threat detection and identification, marking of enemy positions, target acquisition, coordination and deconfliction of distributed Join Fires between networked combat vehicles and tanks also inside Manned and Unmanned Teams (MUM-T).

Worldwide annual military spending on robotics rose from US$5.1 billion in 2010 to US$7.5 billion in 2015. Military drones capable of autonomous action are widely considered a useful asset. Many artificial intelligence researchers seek to distance themselves from military applications of Artificial intelligence.

Audit

For financial statements audit, Artificial intelligence makes continuous audit possible. Artificial intelligence tools could analyze many sets of different information immediately. The potential benefit would be the overall audit risk will be reduced, the level of assurance will be increased and the time duration of audit will be reduced.

Advertising

It is possible to use Artificial intelligence to predict or generalize the behaviour of customers from their digital footprints in order to target them with personalized promotions or build customer personas automatically. A documented case reports that online gambling companies were using AI to improve customer targeting.

Moreover, the application of Personality computing Artificial intelligence models can help to reduce the cost of advertising campaigns by adding psychological targeting to more traditional sociodemographic or behavioural targeting.

Art

Artificial Intelligence has inspired numerous creative applications including its usage to produce visual art. The exhibition "Thinking Machines: Art and Design in the Computer Age, 1959–1989" at MoMA provides a good overview of the historical applications of Artificial intelligence for art, architecture, and design. Recent exhibitions showcasing the usage of AI to produce art include the Google-sponsored benefit and auction at the Gray Area Foundation in San Francisco, where artists experimented with the deep dream algorithm and the exhibition "Unhuman: Art in the Age of Artificial intelligence," which took place in Los Angeles and Frankfurt in the fall of 2017. In the spring of 2018, the Association of Computing Machinery dedicated a special magazine issue to the subject of computers and art highlighting the role of machine learning in the arts. The Austrian Ars Electronica and Museum of Applied Arts, Vienna opened exhibitions on AI in 2019. The Ars Electronica's 2019 festival "Out of the box" extensively thematized the role of arts for a sustainable societal transformation with Artificial intelligence.

PHILOSOPHY OF ARTIFICIAL INTELLIGENCE

There are three philosophical questions related to AI:

1. Is artificial general intelligence possible? Can a machine solve any problem that a human being can solve using intelligence? Or are there hard limits to what a machine can accomplish?

2. Are intelligent machines dangerous? How can we ensure that machines behave ethically and that they are used ethically?

3. Can a machine have a mind, consciousness and mental states in exactly the same sense that human beings do? Can a machine be sentient, and thus deserve certain rights? Can a machine intentionally cause harm?

The limits of artificial general intelligence

Main articles: Philosophy of AI, Turing test, Physical symbol systems hypothesis, Dreyfus' critique of AI, The Emperor's New Mind, and AI effect

Can a machine be intelligent? Can it "think"?

Alan Turing's "polite convention"

We need not decide if a machine can "think"; we need only decide if a machine can act as intelligently as a human being. This approach to the philosophical problems associated with artificial intelligence forms the basis of the Turing test.

The Dartmouth proposal

"Every aspect of learning or any other feature of intelligence can be so precisely described that a machine can be made to simulate it." This conjecture was printed in the proposal for the Dartmouth Conference of 1956.

Newell and Simon's physical symbol system hypothesis

"A physical symbol system has the necessary and sufficient means of general intelligent action." Newell and Simon argue that intelligence consists of formal operations on symbols. Hubert Dreyfus argued that, on the contrary, human expertise depends on unconscious instinct rather than conscious symbol manipulation and on having a "feel" for the situation rather than explicit symbolic knowledge. (See Dreyfus' critique of AI.)

Gödelian arguments

Gödel himself, John Lucas (in 1961) and Roger Penrose (in a more detailed argument from 1989 onwards) made highly technical arguments that human mathematicians can consistently see the truth of their own "Gödel statements" and therefore have computational abilities beyond that of mechanical Turing machines. However, some people do not agree with the "Gödelian arguments".

The artificial brain argument

The brain can be simulated by machines and because brains are intelligent, simulated brains must also be intelligent; thus machines can be intelligent. Hans Moravec, Ray Kurzweil and others have argued that it is technologically feasible to copy the brain directly into hardware and software and that such a simulation will be essentially identical to the original.

The AI effect

Machines are already intelligent, but observers have failed to recognize it. When Deep Blue beat Garry Kasparov in chess, the machine was acting intelligently. However, onlookers commonly discount the behaviour of an artificial intelligence program by arguing that it is not "real" intelligence after all; thus "real" intelligence is whatever intelligent behaviour people can do that machines still cannot. This is known as the AI Effect: "AI is whatever hasn't been done yet."

Potential harm

Widespread use of artificial intelligence could have unintended consequences that are dangerous or undesirable. Scientists from the Future of Life Institute, among others, described some short-term research goals to see how AI influences the economy, the laws and ethics that are involved with AI and how to minimize AI security risks. In the long-term, the scientists have proposed to continue optimizing function while minimizing possible security risks that come along with new technologies.

The potential negative effects of AI and automation are a major issue for Andrew Yang's presidential campaign.

Existential risk

Main article: Existential risk from artificial general intelligence

Physicist Stephen Hawking, Microsoft founder Bill Gates, and SpaceX founder Elon Musk have expressed concerns about the possibility that AI could evolve to the point that humans could not control it, with Hawking theorizing that this could "spell the end of the human race".

The development of full artificial intelligence could spell the end of the human race. Once humans develop artificial intelligence, it will take off on its own and redesign itself at an ever-increasing rate. Humans, who are limited by slow biological evolution, couldn't compete and would be superseded.

Concern over risk from artificial intelligence has led to some high-profile donations and investments. A group of prominent tech titans including Peter Thiel, Amazon Web Services and

Musk have committed $1billion to OpenAI, a nonprofit company aimed at championing responsible AI development. The opinion of experts within the field of artificial intelligence is mixed, with sizable fractions both concerned and unconcerned by risk from eventual superhumanly-capable AI. Other technology industry leaders believe that artificial intelligence is helpful in its current form and will continue to assist humans. Oracle CEO Mark Hurd has stated that AI "will actually create more jobs, not less jobs" as humans will be needed to manage AI systems. Facebook CEO Mark Zuckerberg believes AI will "unlock a huge amount of positive things," such as curing disease and increasing the safety of autonomous cars.

In January 2015, Elon Musk donated ten million dollars to the Future of Life Institute to fund research on understanding AI decision making. The goal of the institute is to "grow wisdom with which we manage" the growing power of technology. Musk also funds companies developing artificial intelligence such as Google DeepMind and Vicarious to "just keep an eye on what's going on with artificial intelligence. I think there is potentially a dangerous outcome there."

For this danger to be realized, the hypothetical AI would have to overpower or out-think all of humanity, which a minority of experts argue is a possibility far enough in the future to not be worth researching. Other counterarguments revolve around humans being either intrinsically or convergently valuable from the perspective of an artificial intelligence.

Devaluation of humanity

Joseph Weizenbaum wrote that AI applications cannot, by definition, successfully simulate genuine human empathy and that the use of AI technology in fields such as customer service or psychotherapy was deeply misguided. Weizenbaum was also bothered that AI researchers (and some philosophers) were willing to view the human mind as nothing more than a computer program (a position now known as computationalism).

To Weizenbaum, these points suggest that AI research devalues human life.

Social justice

One concern is that AI programs may be programmed to be biased against certain groups, such as women and minorities, because most of the developers are wealthy Caucasian men. Support for artificial intelligence is higher among men (with 47% approving) than women (35% approving).

Algorithms have a host of applications in today's legal system already, assisting officials ranging from judges to parole officers and public defenders in gauging the predicted likelihood of recidivism of defendants. COMPAS (an acronym for Correctional Offender Management Profiling for Alternative Sanctions) counts among the most widely utilized commercially available solutions. It has been suggested that COMPAS assigns an exceptionally elevated risk of recidivism to black defendants while, conversely, ascribing low-risk estimate to white defendants significantly more often than statistically expected.

Decrease in demand for human labour

The relationship between automation and employment is complicated. While automation eliminates old jobs, it also creates new jobs through micro-economic and macro-economic effects. Unlike previous waves of automation, many middle-class jobs may be eliminated by artificial intelligence; The Economist states that "the worry that AI could do to white-collar jobs what steam power did to blue-collar ones during the Industrial Revolution" is "worth taking seriously". Subjective estimates of the risk vary widely; for example, Michael Osborne and Carl Benedikt Frey estimate 47% of U.S. jobs are at "high risk" of potential automation, while an OECD report classifies only 9% of U.S. jobs as "high risk". Jobs at extreme risk range from paralegals to fast food cooks, while job demand is likely to increase for care-related professions ranging from personal healthcare to the clergy. Author Martin Ford and others go further and argue that many jobs are routine, repetitive and (to an AI) predictable; Ford warns that these jobs may be automated in the next couple of decades, and that many of the new jobs may not be "accessible to people with average capability", even with retraining. Economists point out that in the past technology has tended to increase rather than reduce total employment, but acknowledge that "we're in uncharted territory" with Artificial intelligence.

Autonomous weapons

Currently, 50+ countries are researching battlefield robots, including the United States, China, Russia, and the United Kingdom. Many people concerned about risk from superintelligent AI also want to limit the use of artificial soldiers and drones.

Ethical machines

Machines with intelligence have the potential to use their intelligence to prevent harm and minimize the risks; they may have the ability to use ethical reasoning to better choose their actions in the world. Research in this area includes machine ethics, artificial moral agents, friendly AI and discussion towards building a human rights framework is also in talks.

Artificial moral agents

Wendell Wallach introduced the concept of artificial moral agents (AMA) in his book Moral Machines For Wallach, AMAs have become a part of the research landscape of artificial intelligence as guided by its two central questions which he identifies as "Does Humanity Want Computers Making Moral Decisions" and "Can (Ro)bots Really Be Moral". For Wallach, the question is not centered on the issue of whether machines can demonstrate the equivalent of moral behaviour in contrast to the constraints which society may place on the development of AMAs.

Machine ethics

The field of machine ethics is concerned with giving machines ethical principles, or a procedure for discovering a way to resolve the ethical dilemmas they might encounter, enabling them to function in an ethically responsible manner through their own ethical decision making. The field was delineated in the AAAI Fall 2005 Symposium on Machine Ethics: "Past research concerning the relationship between technology and ethics has largely focused on responsible and irresponsible use of technology by human beings, with a few people being interested in how human beings ought to treat machines. In all cases, only human beings have engaged in ethical reasoning. The time has come for adding an ethical dimension to at least some machines. Recognition of the ethical ramifications of behaviour involving machines, as well as recent and potential developments in imachine autonomy, necessitate this. In contrast to computer hacking, software property issues, privacy issues and other topics normally ascribed to computer ethics, machine ethics is concerned with the behaviour of machines towards human users and other machines. Research in machine ethics is key to alleviating concerns with iautonomous systems—it could be argued that the notion of autonomous machines without such a dimension is at the root of all fear concerning machine intelligence. Further, the investigation of machine ethics could enable the discovery of iproblems with current ethical theories, advancing our thinking about Ethics." Machine ethics is sometimes referred to as machine morality, computational ethics or computational morality. A variety of perspectives of this nascent field can be found in the collected edition "Machine Ethics" that stems from the AAAI Fall 2005 Symposium on Machine Ethics.

Malevolent and friendly Artificial intelligence

Political scientist Charles T. Rubin believes that AI can be neither designed nor guaranteed to be benevolent. He argues that "any sufficiently advanced benevolence may be indistinguishable from malevolence." Humans should not assume machines or robots would treat us favourably because there is no a priori reason to believe that they would be sympathetic to our system of morality, which has evolved along with our particular biology (which AIs would not share). Hyper-intelligent software may not necessarily decide to support the continued existence of humanity and would be extremely difficult to stop. This topic has also recently begun to be discussed in academic publications as a real source of risks to civilization, humans, and planet Earth.

One proposal to deal with this is to ensure that the first generally intelligent Artificial intelligence is 'Friendly AI' and will be able to control subsequently developed AIs. Some question whether this kind of check could actually remain in place.

Leading AI researcher Rodney Brooks writes, "I think it is a mistake to be worrying about us developing malevolent AI anytime in the next few hundred years. I think the worry stems from a fundamental error in not distinguishing the difference between the very real recent advances in a particular aspect of Artificial intelligence, and the enormity and complexity of building sentient volitional intelligence."

Machine consciousness, sentience and mind

If an Artificial intelligence system replicates all key aspects of human intelligence, will that system also be sentient—will it have a mind which has conscious experiences? This question is closely related to the philosophical problem as to the nature of human consciousness, generally referred to as the hard problem of consciousness.

Consciousness

David Chalmers identified two problems in understanding the mind, which he named the "hard" and "easy" problems of consciousness. The easy problem is understanding how the brain processes signals, makes plans and controls behaviour. The hard problem is explaining how this feels or why it should feel like anything at all. Human information processing is easy to explain, however, human subjective experience is difficult to explain.

For example, consider what happens when a person is shown a colour swatch and identifies it, saying "it's red". The easy problem only requires understanding the machinery in the brain that makes it possible for a person to know that the colour swatch is red. The hard problem is that people also know something else—they also know what red looks like. (Consider that a person born blind can know that something is red without knowing what red looks like.)[l] Everyone knows subjective experience exists, because they do it every day (e.g., all sighted people know what red looks like). The hard problem is explaining how the brain creates it, why it exists, and how it is different from knowledge and other aspects of the brain.

Computationalism and functionalism

Computationalism is the position in the philosophy of mind that the human mind or the human brain (or both) is an information processing system and that thinking is a form of computing. iComputationalism argues that the relationship between mind and body is similar or identical to the relationship between software and hardware and thus may be a solution to the mind-body problem. This philosophical position was inspired by the work of AI researchers and cognitive scientists in the 1960s and was originally proposed by philosophers Jerry Fodor and Hilary Putnam.

Strong Artificial intelligence hypothesis

The philosophical position that John Searle has named "strong Artificial intelligence" states: "The appropriately programmed computer with the right inputs and outputs would thereby have a mind in exactly the same sense human beings have minds." Searle counters this assertion with his Chinese room argument, which asks us to look inside the computer and try to find where the "mind" might be.

Robot rights

If a machine can be created that has intelligence, could it also feel? If it can feel, does it have the same rights as a human? This issue, now known as "robot rights", is currently being considered by, for example, California's Institute for the Future, although many critics believe that the discussion is premature. Some critics of transhumanism argue that any hypothetical robot rights would lie on a spectrum with animal rights and human rights. The subject is profoundly discussed in the 2010 documentary film Plug & Pray, and many sci-fi media such as Star Trek Next Generation, with the character of Commander Data, who fought being disassembled for research, and wanted to "become human", and the robotic holograms in Voyager.

Superintelligence

Are there limits to how intelligent machines or human-machine hybrids can be? A superintelligence, hyperintelligence, or superhuman intelligence is a hypothetical agent that would possess intelligence far surpassing that of the brightest and most gifted human mind. Superintelligence may also refer to the form or degree of intelligence possessed by such an agent.

Technological singularity

If research into Strong AI produced sufficiently intelligent software, it might be able to reprogram and improve itself. The improved software would be even better at improving itself, leading to recursive self-improvement. The new intelligence could thus increase exponentially and dramatically surpass humans. Science fiction writer Vernor Vinge named this scenario "singularity". Technological singularity is when accelerating progress in technologies will cause a runaway effect wherein artificial intelligence will exceed human intellectual capacity and control, thus radically changing or even ending civilization. Because the capabilities of such an intelligence may be impossible to comprehend, the technological singularity is an occurrence beyond which events are unpredictable or even unfathomable.

Ray Kurzweil has used Moore's law (which describes the relentless exponential improvement in digital technology) to calculate that desktop computers will have the same processing power as human brains by the year 2029, and predicts that the singularity will occur in 2045.

Transhumanism

Robot designer Hans Moravec, cyberneticist Kevin Warwick and inventor Ray Kurzweil have predicted that humans and machines will merge in the future into cyborgs that are more capable and powerful than either. This idea, called transhumanism, has roots in Aldous Huxley and Robert Ettinger.

Edward Fredkin argues that "artificial intelligence is the next stage in evolution", an idea first proposed by Samuel Butler's "Darwin among the Machines" as far back as 1863, and expanded upon by George Dyson in his book of the same name in 1998.

GOALS OF ARTIFICIAL INTELLIGENCE

To Create Expert Systems: The systems which exhibit intelligent behaviour, learn, demonstrate, explain, and advise its users. To Implement Human Intelligence in Machines: Creating systems that understand, think, learn, and behave like humans.

Elevator Pitch

Simply said: Artificial intelligence (AI) is the ability of a computer program or a machine to think as humans do.

AI is using technology to do things which used to require human intelligence, for example, problem-solving or learning, and will likely shape our future more than any technology that has come before.

Machine learning (ML) is a subfield of AI and gives machines the skills to 'learn' from examples without being explicitly programmed to do so. Deep learning (DL) is a specialized ML technique that mimics the behaviour of the human brain and enables machines to train themselves to perform tasks.

Artificial intelligence is the goal; Artificial intelligence is the planet we're headed to. Machine learning is the rocket that's going to get us there. And Big Data is the fuel.

As should be clear from the above, machines are increasingly getting smarter and are picking up more and more tasks which could previously only be done by humans.

A lot of people, therefore, have this misconception that artificial intelligence was designed to replace humans and whatever we do in our daily work or at home. However, AI was (and is being) developed for the sole purpose of augmenting our lives and amplifying our skills and capabilities in all that we do. We are entering an age where man and machine will collaborate ever more closely. Many countries have published or announced national AI strategies to capitalize on the technology's potential and become a global leader.

Core concepts

Machine learning (ML) is a subfield of AI and is its most common application. A computer system is fed data which it uses to recognize patterns and make decisions or predictions without being explicitly programmed.

Think for example of understanding speech or automatically classifying an email as 'spam' or 'non-spam'. Machine learning is one of the most desirable IT skills today.

Deep learning (DL) is a subfield of ML and is the hot topic of the day as it aims to simulate human thinking. It basically is machine learning on steroids and allows the crunching of vast amounts of data with improved accuracy. As it's more powerful it also requires considerably more computing power.

Algorithms can determine on their own (without the intervention of an engineer) whether a prediction is accurate or not. Think for example of providing an algorithm with thousands of images and videos of cats and dogs. It can look at whether the animal has whiskers, paws or a furry tail, and use learnings to predict whether new data fed into the system is more likely to be a cat or a dog.

There are three main algorithms or techniques you should be aware of:

Supervised learning – You are given a training data set with clearly defined labels and thus already know the 'right answers'. The algorithm will help provide more of the same answers. Supervised learning is for example used to classify an email as spam or non-spam and to detect fraud.

Unsupervised learning – You are not given a training data set, but only have input data which has not been labelled/categorized, yet the algorithm must automatically try to find patterns. The model will cluster data based on relationships among the variables.

Unsupervised learning is where you'll hear most of the excitement when people talk about 'the future of AI' due to its limitless potential. It's for example used for market segmentation (i.e. clustering groups of customers based on common characteristics) and to provide product recommendations based on a shopper's historical purchase behaviour.

Reinforcement learning – An algorithm interacts with a dynamic environment in which it must perform a certain goal, like driving a car, without a teacher explicitly telling it whether it has come close to its goal. For each action it takes, a reward (positive or negative) is received. The goal is to find the best actions which maximize the long-term reward. The algorithm thus learns by trial and error. An example is learning to play a computer game by playing against an opponent.

Big data acts as an ingredient. Think of it as when you are making a cake – the data represents the flour and the actual process of baking the cake is represented through machine learning. Artificial intelligence will then be the output, or the cake if you will.

Key Benefits

- **Improve decision making**

Artificial intelligence enables speed and accuracy levels previously impossible. We are experiencing massive growth in unstructured data from numerous sources from an always-on consumer. The ability to highlight non-obvious relationships in these data sets due to rapid data processing and analysis drastically improves decision making at scale. This will help organizations with future planning as they can learn from past behaviours and act in real-time.

- **Hyper-personalization**

Besides allowing for hidden pattern analysis and better prediction models, automated learning enables hyper-personalization. Use cases go from marketing to a segment of one (the holy grail of every marketer) to areas such as personalized food and precision medicine.

- **Business process optimization**

Increased productivity and operational efficiencies are key reasons behind the widespread adoption of AI. Using advanced modelling and simulation techniques, machine learning can assess automated processes in the organization and make any adjustments in real-time.

- **Free up time for more substantive and creative work**

Mundane tasks that do not require time to think will be automated first. This could lead to a reduced headcount while time gains will result in important cost savings. Improved labour productivity as a result of AI investments will give employees the opportunity to focus on more creative and value-adding work.

Whilst the efficient analysis of big data sets and more 'objective' decision-making will be the main advantage of artificial intelligence, there is a long road ahead to solve for the bias problem of algorithms. You may have heard of Microsoft's racist chatbot Tay which took a turn for the vulgar in less than 24 hours on Twitter, or the case of risk assessment software COMPAS which predicted blacks were twice as likely as whites to be labelled a higher risk of recidivism.

The main problem is that we humans are inherently biased. AI hence reflects and augments all of our society's assumptions and perceptions – good or bad.

With Artificial intelligence increasingly being used in the hiring process and in fare pricing by companies such as Uber and Lyft, prejudice needs to be tackled head-on if consumer trust is ever to be gained.

How Artificial Intelligence is disrupting industries

Artificial intelligence (AI) and machine learning (ML) have wide applicability, going from your Netflix content recommendations to detecting fraud with PayPal and even allowing drones to fly autonomously.

Let's look at the role they are playing as the next big industry disruptors.

- **Financial Services**

Banking and insurance are leading the way in the adoption of artificial intelligence. FinTech and InsurTech are disrupting the industry helping reduce administration time and automate back-office operations.

A popular use of AI you might be familiar with is the personal digital assistant. Chatbots and voice assistants are being used to provide 24/7 customer service and let customers check their account balances and make money transfers.

Active.ai and Finn.ai are some of the platforms specialized in developing these virtual assistant solutions for financial institutions.

Robo-advisors like Betterment simplify investing and wealth management and make such services more accessible to a wider population, while HSBC is using AI to prevent fraud and money laundering by spotting abnormalities in transactions.

- **Retail**

The use of AI in retail is heavily focused on providing a better in-store and online customer experience. Extreme personalization is made possible due to the real-time analysis of big volumes of data.

Besides virtual assistants and voice-based shopping, artificial intelligence is being used by retailers like H&M to predict the next big fashion trends and customize their store offering.

Other AI use cases address bottlenecks in the supply chain such as inventory management, demand forecasting and automatic product replenishment. German retailer Otto is, for example, partnering with Blue Yonder for price optimization and reducing their out-of-stock rates.

For an in-depth look at how artificial intelligence and other exponential technologies are disrupting the retail industry, go here.

- **Automotive**

One of the most prominent examples of the use of artificial intelligence can be found in assisted and autonomous driving. Every big car manufacturer is heavily investing in AI to improve driver safety by automating the detection of pedestrians and road signage and creating the ability to anticipate and course correct when something goes wrong.

Affectiva launched Automotive AI, a platform which can sense driver fatigue, anger or distraction and alert or intervene accordingly. In-car music can be personalized, and lighting and heating can be adapted based on the analysis of facial and vocal expressions of passengers.

- **Healthcare**

Intelligent diagnostics is a game-changer in the medical industry. Its main power lies in the ability to analyze vast amounts of information such as medical history and genetic information across systems inside and outside the healthcare organization. AI has already proven to be better than dermatologists at detecting skin cancer and can spot Alzheimer a decade before human doctors. Equipped with AI, your Apple Watch can even predict heart problems and detect diabetes.

Pharmaceutical giant Pfizer is developing a drug discovery platform, while LG Health and Aspire have launched a $300 million fund to fast-track the development of precision medicine. Machine learning algorithms are incredibly powerful tools that can learn the rules of drug design to improve existing drugs or develop new ones.

Besides increasing the speed and accuracy of treatments, artificial intelligence will play an important role in providing superior patient care. Voice-enabled healthcare assistants like Suki already help lift the burden of medical documentation so that doctors can actually focus on taking care of their patients. Any improvements in misdiagnosis and more efficient drug development will significantly reduce the cost of healthcare.

Check out all areas where Artificial intelligence is challenging doctors on their home turf.

- **HR & Recruitment**

AI and machine learning can be used to automate some of the mundane and repetitive tasks of recruitment and reduce a typically lengthy hiring process.

Startups like Reminder ease the sourcing and screening of job applications with an attempt to surface unusual candidates and prevent recruiting bias.

Textio augments the writing of job posts and direct candidate communications. Unilever even sets up digital interviews to screen entry-level employees using facial recognition and keyword analysis. The latter is a specifically interesting domain with a few companies now entering the playing field, for example, Searchie which has a live virtual assistant who interviews candidates and provides a detailed assessment in minutes.

In this increasingly data-driven world, the importance and impact of artificial intelligence is only growing and is becoming more crucial in gaining competitive advantage. AI as a service (AIaaS) is helping democratize AI and provides small and large businesses equal access to high-quality training data and expertise with less risk and lower cost.

Regardless of the above and all the AI news clogging your inbox, it's important to understand that while AI might be the future, we should never lose sight of the human touch.

Glossary

- **Artificial Narrow Intelligence (ANI)**

AI specialized in one field in which it can outperform a human, such as playing a game of chess or Jeopardy or performing isurgery.

- **Artificial General Intelligence (AGI)**

A state where imachines are equally intelligent to humans in every aspect.

- **Artificial Super Intelligence (ASI)**

A state where AI is vastly superior to the best human brains in every field.

- **Supervised learning**

The machine learning task of training a model on a pre-defined data set consisting of input and desired output values (data labels). This allows an algorithm to provide accurate decisions when new data is provided.

- **Unsupervised learning**

The machine learning task of identifying hidden structures from 'unlabeled' data. Examples include clustering (where we try to idiscover underlying groupings of examples) and anomaly detection (where we try to infer if some examples in a dataset do not conform to some expected pattern).

- **Reinforcement learning**

    Learning through trial and error. A computer program interacts with a dynamic environment in which it must perform a certain goal (e.g. idriving a vehicle) without a teacher explicitly telling it whether it has come close to its goal.

- **Neural networks**

    A type of machine learning model that builds up complex models by connecting simple units (neurons). Each unit is linked to other units in the network and influence the 'activation' of these other units.

- **Training example**

    A combination of some input data (e.g. the area of a house) and some output data (e.g. the price of a house) that we are trying to predict using a model.

- **Training set**

    The set of examples a model is trained on.

- **Turing test**

    A test named after computer science pioneer Alan Turing to determine whether a machine is capable of thinking like a human. If an examiner cannot distinguish a response from a machine from that of a human, the test is passed.

- **Natural Language Processing (NLP)**

    The ability for a computer or system to understand and process human language as it is spoken. NLP is an area of AI.

INTELLIGENT iSYSTEMS

While studying artificial intelligence, you need to know what intelligence is. This chapter covers the Idea of intelligence, types, and components of intelligence.

What is Intelligence?

The ability of a system to calculate, reason, perceive relationships and analogies, learn from experience, store and retrieve information from memory, solve problems, comprehend complex ideas, use natural language fluently, classify, generalize, and adapt new situations.

Types of Intelligence

As described by Howard Gardner, an American developmental psychologist, the Intelligence comes in multifold:

Intelligence	Description	Example
Linguistic Intelligence	The ability to speak, recognize, and use mechanisms of phonology (speech sounds), syntax (grammar), and semantics (meaning).	Narrators, Orators
Musical Intelligence	The ability to create, communicate with and understand meanings made of sound.	Musicians, Singers, Composers

Logical-mathematical intelligence	The ability to use and understand relationships in the absence of action or objects. Understanding complex and abstract ideas.	Mathematicians, Scientists
Spatial Intelligence	The ability to perceive visual or spatial information, change it, and re-create visual images without reference to the objects, construct 3D images, and to move and rotate them.	Map readers, Astronauts, Physicists
Bodily-Kinesthetic Intelligence	The ability to use complete or part of the body to solve problems or fashion products, control over fine and coarse motor skills, and manipulate the objects.	Players, Dancers

Intra-personal Intelligence	The ability to distinguish among one's own feelings, intentions, and motivations.	Gautam Buddha
Interpersonal Intelligence	The ability to recognize and make distinctions among other people's feelings, beliefs, and intentions.	Mass Communicators, Interviewers

You can say a machine or a system is artificially intelligent when it is equipped with at least one and at most all intelligence in it.

What iis iIntelligence iComposed iof?

The intelligence is intangible. It is composed of:

1. Reasoning
2. Learning
3. Problem Solving
4. Perception
5. Linguistic Intelligence

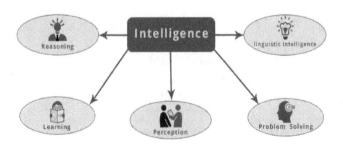

Let us go through iall ithe icomponents briefly:

1 **Reasoning:** It is the set of processes that enables us to provide a basis for judgement, making decisions, and prediction. There are broadly two types:

Inductive Reasoning	Deductive Reasoning
It conducts specific observations to makes broad general statements.	It starts with a general statement and examines the possibilities to reach a specific, logical conclusion.
Even if all of the premises are true in a statement, inductive reasoning allows for the conclusion to be false.	If something is true of a class of things in general, it is also true for all members of that class.
Example: "Nina is a teacher. All teachers are studious. Therefore, Nina is studious."	Example: "All women of age above 60 years are grandmothers. Shelan is 65 years. Therefore, Shelan is a grandmother."

1. **Learning:** It is the activity of gaining knowledge or skill by studying, practising, being taught, or experiencing something. Learning enhances the awareness of the subjects of the study.

2. The ability of learning is possessed by humans, some animals, and AI-enabled systems. Learning is categorized as:

3. **Auditory Learning:** It is learning by listening and hearing. For example, students listening to recorded audio lectures.

4. **Episodic Learning:** To learn by remembering sequences of events that one has witnessed or experienced. This is linear and orderly.

5. **Motor Learning:** It is learning by the precise movement of muscles. For example, picking objects, Writing, etc.

6. **Observational Learning:** To learn by watching and imitating others. For example, a child tries to learn by mimicking her parent.

7. **Perceptual Learning:** It is learning to recognize stimuli that one has seen before. For example, identifying and classifying objects and situations.

8. **Relational Learning:** It involves learning to differentiate among various stimuli on the basis of relational properties, rather than absolute properties. For Example,

9. Adding 'little less' salt at the time of cooking potatoes that came up salty last time, when cooked with adding say a tablespoon of salt.

10. **Spatial learning:** It is learning through visual stimuli such as images, colours, maps, etc. For Example, A person can create a roadmap in mind before actually following the road.

11. **Stimulus-Response Learning:** It is learning to perform a particular behaviour when a certain stimulus is present. For example, a dog raises its ear on the hearing doorbell.

12. **Problem solving:** It is the process in which one perceives and tries to arrive at the desired solution from a present situation by taking some path, which is blocked by known or unknown hurdles.

13. Problem solving also includes decision making, which is the process of selecting the best suitable alternative out

of multiple alternatives to reach the desired goal are available.

14. **Perception:** It is the process of acquiring, interpreting, selecting, and organizing sensory information.

15. Perception presumes sensing. In humans, perception is aided by sensory organs. In the domain of AI, perception mechanism puts the data acquired by the sensors together in a meaningful manner.

16. **Linguistic Intelligence:** It is one's ability to use, comprehend, speak, and write the verbal and written language. It is important in interpersonal communication.

Difference between Human and Machine Intelligence

Everyone knows that humans and machines are different. Machines are the creation of humans, and they were created to make their work easier. Humans depend more and more on machines for their day-to-day things. Machines have created a revolution, and no human can think of a life without machines.

A machine is only a device consisting of different parts and is used for performing different functions. They do not have life, as they are mechanical. On the other hand, humans are made of flesh and blood; life is just not mechanical for humans.

Humans have feelings and emotions, and they can express these emotions; happiness and sorrow are part of one's life. On the other hand, machines have no feelings and emotions. They just work as per the details fed into their mechanical brain. Humans have the capability to understand situations and behave accordingly. On the contrary, Machines do not have this capability.

While humans behave according to their consciousness, machines perform as they are taught. Humans perform activities as per their own intelligence. On the contrary, machines only have artificial intelligence. It is a man-made intelligence that the machines have. The brilliance of the intelligence of a machine depends on the intelligence of the humans that created it.

Another striking difference that can be seen is that humans can do anything original, and machines cannot. Machines have limitations to their performance because they need humans to guide them.

Though machines are very sophisticated, they cannot perform anything original. Machines do not have original thoughts. Another thing that has to be noted is that machines are not superior to humans.

Summary:

1. Humans perceive by patterns whereas the machines perceive by a set of rules and data.

2. Humans store and recall information by patterns, machines do it by searching algorithms. For example, the number 40404040 is easy to remember, store and recall as its pattern is simple.

3. Humans can figure out the complete object even if some part of it is missing or distorted; whereas the machines cannot correctly.

4. Machines do not have life, as they are mechanical. On the other hand, humans are made of flesh and blood; life is not mechanical for humans.

5. Humans have feelings and emotions, and they can express these emotions. Machines have no feelings and emotions. They just work as per the details fed into their mechanical brain.

6. Humans can do anything original, and machines cannot.

7. Humans have the capability to understand situations and behave accordingly. On the contrary, machines do not have this capability.

8. While humans behave as per their consciousness, machines just perform as they are taught.

9. Humans perform activities as per their own intelligence. On the contrary, machines only have an artificial intelligence

EXPERT SYSTEMS

In artificial intelligence, an expert system is a computer system that emulates the decision-making ability of a human expert. Expert systems are designed to solve complex problems by reasoning through bodies of knowledge, represented mainly as if-then rules rather than through conventional procedural code. The first expert systems were created in the 1970s and then proliferated in the 1980s. Expert systems were among the first truly successful forms of artificial intelligence (AI) software. An expert system is divided into two subsystems: the inference engine and the knowledge base. The knowledge base represents facts and rules. The inference engine applies the rules to the known facts to deduce new facts. Inference engines can also include an explanation and debugging abilities.

What is an Expert System?

An Expert System is defined as an interactive and reliable computer-based decision-making system which uses both facts and heuristics to solve complex decision-making problems. It is considered at the highest level of human intelligence and expertise. It is a computer application which solves the most complex issues in a specific domain.

The expert system can resolve many issues which generally would require a human expert. It is based on knowledge acquired from an expert. It is also capable of expressing and reasoning about some domain of knowledge. Expert systems were the predecessor of the current day artificial intelligence, deep learning and machine learning systems.

Examples of Expert Systems

Following are iexamples of Expert Systems

- MYCIN: It was based on backward chaining and could identify various bacteria that could cause acute infections. It could also recommend drugs based on the patient's weight.

- DENDRAL: Expert system used for chemical analysis to predict molecular structure.

- PXDES: Expert system used to predict the degree and type of lung cancer

- CaDet: Expert system that could identify cancer at early stages

Characteristic of Expert System

Following are Important characteristic of Expert System:

- **The Highest Level of Expertise:** The expert system offers the highest level of expertise. It provides efficiency, accuracy and imaginative problem-solving.

- **Right on Time Reaction:** An Expert System interacts in a very reasonable period of time with the user. The total time must be less than the time taken by an expert to get the most accurate solution for the same problem.

- **Good Reliability:** The expert system needs to be reliable, and it must not make any a mistake.

- **Flexible:** It is vital that it remains flexible as it is possessed by an Expert system.

- **Effective Mechanism:** Expert System must have an efficient mechanism to administer the compilation of the existing knowledge in it.

- **Capable of handling challenging decision & problems:** An expert system is capable of handling challenging decision problems and delivering solutions.

Components of the expert system

The components of expert system include:

- Knowledge Base
- Inference Engine
- User Interface

Let us see them one by one briefly:

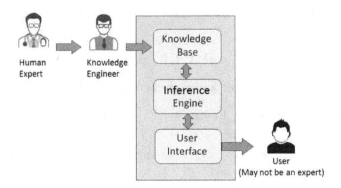

The expert system consists of the following given components:

User Interface

The user interface is the most crucial part of the expert system. This component takes the user's query in a readable form and passes it to the inference engine. After that, it displays the results to the user. In other words, it's an interface that helps the user communicate with the expert system.

Inference Engine

The inference engine is the brain of the expert system. Inference engine contains rules to solve a ispecific problem. It refers to the knowledge from the Knowledge Base. It selects facts and rules to apply when trying to answer the user's query. It provides reasoning about the information in the knowledge base. It also helps in deducting the problem to find the solution. This component is also helpful for formulating conclusions.

Knowledge Base

The knowledge base is a repository of facts. It stores all the knowledge about the problem domain. It is like a large container of knowledge which is obtained from different experts of a specific field.

Thus we can say that the success of the Expert System mainly depends on the highly accurate and precise knowledge.

Other key terms used in Expert systems

Facts and Rules

A fact is a small portion of important information. Facts on their own are of very limited use. The rules are essential to select and apply facts to a user problem.

Knowledge Acquisition

The term knowledge acquisition means how to get the required domain knowledge by the expert system. The entire process starts by extracting knowledge from a human expert, converting the acquired knowledge into rules and injecting the developed rules into the knowledge base.

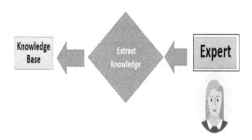

Participant in Expert Systems Development

Participant	Role
Domain Expert	He is a person or group whose expertise and knowledge is taken to develop an expert system.
Knowledge Engineer	A knowledge engineer is a technical person who integrates knowledge into computer systems.
End-User	It is a person or group of people who are using the expert system to get to get advice which will not be provided by the expert.

The process of Building An Expert Systems

- Determining the characteristics of the problem

- Knowledge engineer and domain expert work in coherence to define the problem

- The knowledge engineer translates the knowledge into a computer-understandable language. He designs an inference engine, a reasoning structure, which can use knowledge when needed.

- Knowledge Expert also determines how to integrate the use of uncertain knowledge in the reasoning process and what type of explanation would be useful.

Conventional System vs. Expert system

Conventional System	Expert System
Knowledge and processing are combined in one unit.	Knowledge database and the processing mechanism are two separate components.
The programme does not make errors (Unless error in programming).	The Expert System may make a mistake.
The system is operational only when fully developed.	The expert system is optimized on an ongoing basis and can be launched with a small number of rules.
Step by step execution according to fixed algorithms is required.	Execution is done logically & heuristically.
It needs full information.	It can be functional with sufficient or insufficient information.

Human expert vs. expert system

Human Expert	Artificial Expertise
Perishable	Permanent
Difficult to Transfer	Transferable
Difficult to Document	Easy to Document
Unpredictable	Consistent
Expensive	Cost-effective System

Benefits of expert systems

- It improves the decision quality
- Cuts the expense of consulting experts for problem-solving

- It provides fast and efficient solutions to problems in a narrow area of specialization.

- It can gather scarce expertise and used it efficiently.

- Offers consistent answer for the repetitive problem

- Maintains a significant level of information

- Helps you to get fast and accurate answers

- A proper explanation of decision making

- Ability to solve complex and challenging issues

Expert Systems can work steadily work without getting emotional, tensed or fatigued. Limitations of the expert system

- Unable to make a creative response in an extraordinary situation

- Errors in the knowledge base can lead to wrong decision

- The maintenance cost of an expert system is too expensive

- Each problem is different therefore the solution from a human expert can also be different and more creative

Applications of expert systems

Some popular application where expert systems user:

- Information management

- Hospitals and medical facilities

- Help desks management

- Employee performance evaluation

- Loan analysis

- Virus detection

- Useful for repair and maintenance projects

- Warehouse optimization

- Planning and scheduling

- The configuration of manufactured objects

- Financial decision making Knowledge publishing

- Process monitoring and control

- Supervise the operation of the plant and controller

- Stock market trading

- Airline scheduling & cargo schedules

Summary

- An Expert System is an interactive and reliable computer-based decision-making system which uses both facts and heuristics to solve complex decision-making problem

- Key components of an Expert System are 1) User Interface, 2) Inference Engine, 3) Knowledge Base

- Key participants in Expert Systems Development are 1) Domain Expert 2) Knowledge Engineer 3) End-User

- Improved decision quality, reduce cost, consistency, reliability, speed are key benefits of an Expert System

- An Expert system cannot give creative solutions and can be costly to maintain.

- An Expert System can be used in broad applications like Stock Market, Warehouse, HR, etc

ARTIFICIAL INTELLIGENCE
RESEARCH AREAS

The working domain of artificial intelligence is huge in width and breadth. Therefore before proceeding further considers uic prospering and common research areas in the domain of artificial intelligence are:

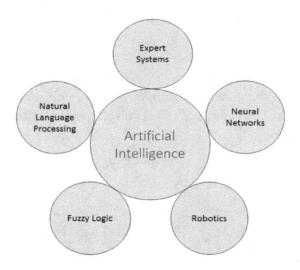

Expert System - In artificial intelligence, an expert system is used for solving complex problems by reasoning about knowledge, represented primarily by if-then rules rather than by conventional procedural code. In general, an expert system is a computer system that uses the decision-making capability of a human expert.

Neural Networks - Neural networks are system of interconnected neurons? which exchange messages between each other. In machine learning artificial neural networks (ANNs) belongs to a family of model inspired by biological neural networks (the nervous system of animals, present inside a brain) and are used for approximate functions or estimate a large number of inputs which are generally unknown.

Robotics - Robotics is a branch of Artificial Intelligence (AI), it is mainly composed of electrical engineering, mechanical engineering and computer science engineering for construction, designing and application of robots. Robotics is the science of building or designing an application of robots. The aim of robotics is to design an efficient robot.

Fuzzy logic - Fuzzy logic was introduced in 1965 as a proposal of fuzzy set theory. It is applied to various fields, from artificial intelligence to control theory. Fuzzy logic is a form of many-valued logic in which truth table values of variable may be real number between 0 and 1.

Natural Language Processing - Natural language processing (NLP) is a method of communicating with an intelligent system by using a natural language such as English. The input and output of NLP system is speech and written text.

Voice and Speech Recognition

Voice and Speech both terms are common in expert systems, natural language processing and robotics. As these terms are used interchangeably, their objectives are different.

The differences between voice and speech recognition are given below:

Voice Recognition	Speech Recognition
The aim of voice recognition is to recognize WHO is speaking.	The aim of speech recognition is to understand and comprehend WHAT was spoken.
This recognition system requires training as it is	This recognition system does not require training as it

person-oriented.	is not speaker-dependent.
It is used for identifying a person by analyzing its voice, tone, pitch, and accent, etc.	It is used for hand-free computing, menu navigation, or map.
Speaker dependent Voice Recognition systems are easy to develop.	Speaker independent Speech Recognition systems are difficult to develop.

Working of Speech and Voice Recognition Systems

The user input spoken at a microphone goes to the sound card of the system. The converter turns the analogue signal into an equivalent digital signal for the speech processing. The database is used to compare the patterns to recognize the words. Finally, a reverse feedback is given to the database.

This source-language text becomes input to the Translation Engine, which converts it to the target language text. They are supported with interactive GUI, large database of vocabulary etc.

Task Classification of Artificial Intelligence

The domain of Artificial Intelligence is classified into Formal tasks, Mundane tasks, and Expert tasks.

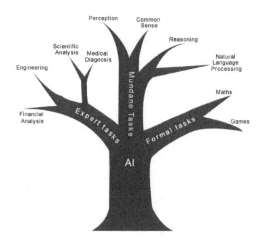

Task Domains of Artificial Intelligence

Mundane (Ordinary) Tasks	Formal Tasks	Expert Tasks
Perception • Computer Vision • Speech, Voice	• Mathematics • Geometry • Logic • Integration and Differentiation	• Engineering • Fault Finding • Manufacturing • Monitoring
Natural Language Processing • Understanding • Language Generation • Language Translation	Games • Go • Chess (Deep Blue) • Checkers	Scientific Analysis
Common Sense	Verification	Financial Analysis

Reasoning	Theorem Proving	Medical Diagnosis
Planing		Creativity
Robotics • Locomotive		

Humans learn mundane (ordinary) tasks since their birth. They learn by perception, speaking, using language, and locomotives. They learn Formal Tasks and Expert Tasks later, in that order.

For humans, the mundane tasks are easiest to learn. The same was considered true before trying to implement mundane tasks in machines. Earlier, all work of AI was concentrated in the mundane task domain.

Later, it turned out that the machine requires more knowledge, complex knowledge representation, and complicated algorithms for handling mundane tasks. This is the reason why AI work is more prospering in the Expert Tasks domain now, as the expert task domain needs expert knowledge without common sense, which can be easier to represent and handle.

AGENTS AND ENVIRONMENTS

An AI system is composed of an agent and its environment. The agents act in their environment. The environment may contain other agents.

What are Agent and Environment?

An agent is anything that can perceive its environment through sensors and acts upon that environment through effectors.

- A human agent has sensory organs such as eyes, ears, nose, tongue and skin parallel to the sensors, and other organs such as hands, legs, mouth, for effectors.

- A robotic agent replaces cameras and infrared range finders for the sensors, and various motors and actuators for effectors.

- A software agent has encoded bit strings as its programs and actions.

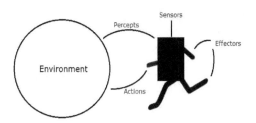

Agents Terminology

- Performance Measure of Agent: It is the criteria, which determines how successful an agent is.

- The behaviour of Agent: It is the action that the agent performs after any given sequence of percepts.

- Percept: It is the agent's perceptual inputs at a given instance.

- Percept Sequence: It is the history of all that an agent has perceived till date.

- Agent Function: It is a map from the precept sequence to an action.

Rationality

Rationality is nothing but the status of being reasonable, sensible, and having a good sense of judgment.

Rationality is concerned with expected actions and results depending upon what the agent has perceived. Performing actions with the aim of obtaining useful information is an important part of rationality.

What is Ideal Rational Agent?

An ideal rational agent is the one, which is capable of doing expected actions to maximize its performance measure, on the basis of:

- Its percept sequence

- Its built-in knowledge base

The rationality of an agent depends on the following:

- The performance measures, which determine the degree of success.

- Agent's Percept Sequence till now.

- The agent's prior knowledge about the environment.

- The actions that the agent can carry out.

A rational agent always performs the right action, where the right action means the action that causes the agent to be most successful in the given percept sequence. The problem the agent solves is characterized by Performance Measure, Environment, Actuators, and Sensors (PEAS).

The Structure of Intelligent Agents

Agent's structure can be viewed as:

- Agent = Architecture + Agent Program

- Architecture = the machinery that an agent executes on.

- Agent Program = an implementation of an agent function.

Simple Reflex Agents

- They choose actions only based on the current percept.

- They are rational only if a correct decision is made only on the basis of current precept.

- Their environment is completely observable.

Condition-Action Rule – It is a rule that maps a state (condition) to an action.

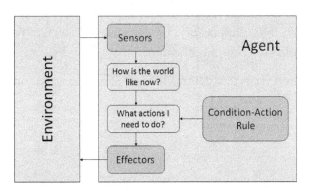

Model-Based Reflex Agents

They use a model of the world to choose their actions. They maintain an internal state.

Model: knowledge about "how things happen in the world".

Internal State: It is a representation of unobserved aspects of the current state depending on percept history.

Updating state requires the information about

- How the world evolves.

- How the agent's actions affect the world.

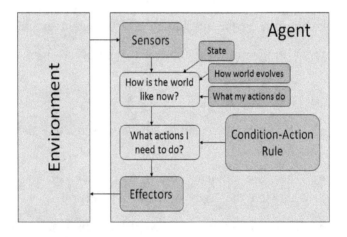

Goal-Based Agents

They choose their actions in order to achieve goals. The goal-based approach is more flexible than a reflex agent since the knowledge supporting a decision is explicitly modelled, thereby allowing for modifications.

- **Goal:** It is the description of desirable situations.

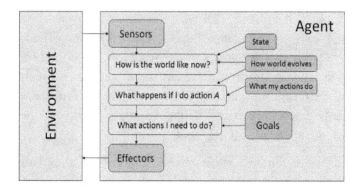

Utility-Based Agents

They choose actions based on preference (utility) for each state.

Goals are inadequate when:

- There are conflicting goals only some of which can be achieved.

- Goals have some uncertainty of being achieved and one needs to weigh the likelihood of success against the importance of a goal.

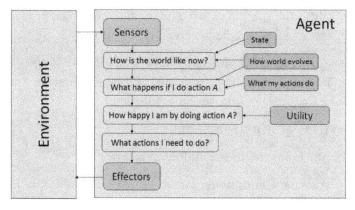

The Nature of Environments

Some programs operate in the entirely artificial environment confined to keyboard input, database, computer file systems and character output on a screen.

In contrast, some software agents (software robots or softbots) exist in rich, unlimited softbots domains. The simulator has a very detailed, complex environment. The software agent needs to choose from a long array of actions in real-time. A softbot designed to scan the online preferences of the customer and show interesting items to the customer works in the real as well as an artificial environment.

The most famous artificial environment is the Turing Test environment, in which one real and other artificial agents are tested on equal ground. This is a very challenging environment as it is highly difficult for a software agent to perform as well as a human.

Turing Test

The success of an intelligent behaviour of a system can be measured with the Turing Test.

Two persons and a machine to be evaluated participate in the test. Out of the two persons, one plays the role of the tester. Each of them sits in different rooms. The tester is unaware of who is a machine and who is a human. He interrogates the questions by typing and sending them to both intelligences, to which he receives typed responses.

This test aims at fooling the tester. If the tester fails to determine the machine's response from the human response, then the machine is said to be intelligent.

Properties of Environment

The environment has multifold properties:

- **Discrete/Continuous:** If there are a limited number of distinct, clearly defined, states of the environment, the environment is discrete (For example, chess); otherwise it is continuous (For example, driving).

- **Observable/Partially Observable:** If it is possible to determine the complete state of the environment at each time point from the percepts it is observable; otherwise it is only partially observable.

- **Static/Dynamic:** If the environment does not change while an agent is acting, then it is static; otherwise it is dynamic.

- **Single-agent/Multiple agents:** The environment may contain other agents which may be of the same or different kind as that of the agent.

- **Accessible vs. inaccessible:** If the agent's sensory apparatus can have access to the complete state of the environment, then the environment is accessible to that agent.

- **Deterministic vs. Non-deterministic:** If the next state of the environment is completely determined by the current state and the actions of the agent, then the environment is deterministic; otherwise it is non-deterministic.

- **Episodic vs. Non-episodic:** In an episodic environment, each episode consists of the agent perceiving and then acting. The quality of its action depends just on the episode itself. Subsequent episodes do not depend on the actions in the previous episodes. Episodic environments are much simpler because the agent does not need to think ahead.

POPULAR SEARCH ALGORITHMS

Searching is the universal technique of problem-solving in AI. There are some single-player games such as tile games, Sudoku, crossword, etc. The search algorithms help you to search for a particular position in such games.

Single Agent Pathfinding Problems

The games such as 3X3 eight-tile, 4X4 fifteen-tile, and 5X5 twenty-four tile puzzles are single-agent-path-finding challenges. They consist of a matrix of tiles with a blank tile. The player is required to arrange the tiles by sliding a tile either vertically or horizontally into blank space with the aim of accomplishing some objective.

The other examples of single-agent pathfinding problems are Travelling Salesman Problem, Rubik's Cube, and Theorem Proving.

Search Terminology

Problem Space: It is the environment in which the search takes place. (A set of states and set of operators to change those states)

Problem Instance: It is Initial state + Goal state

Problem Space Graph: It represents a problem state. States are shown by nodes and operators are shown by edges.

Depth of a problem: Length of the shortest path or shortest sequence of operators from Initial State to goal state.

Space Complexity: The maximum number of nodes that are stored in memory.

Time Complexity: The maximum number of nodes that are created.

Admissibility: A property of an algorithm to always find an optimal solution.

Branching Factor: The average number of child nodes in the problem space graph.

Depth: Length of the shortest path from the initial state to the goal state.

Brute-Force Search Strategies

They are mostly simple, as they do not need any domain-specific knowledge. They work fine with small number of possible states.

Requirements –

- State description
- A set of valid operators
- Initial state
- Goal state description

Breadth-First Search

It starts from the root node, explores the neighbouring nodes first and moves towards the next level neighbours. It generates one tree at a time until the solution is found. It can be implemented using FIFO queue data structure. This method provides the shortest path to the solution.

If branching factor (average number of child nodes for a given node) = b and depth = d, then a number of nodes at level d = bd.

The total no of nodes created in worst case is b + b2 + b3 + ... + bd.

Disadvantage: Since each level of nodes is saved for creating next one, it consumes a lot of memory space. Space requirement to store nodes is exponential.

Its complexity depends on the number of nodes. It can check duplicate nodes.

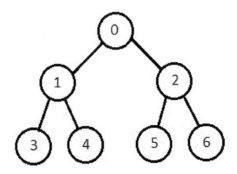

Depth-First Search

It is implemented in recursion with LIFO stack data structure. It creates the same set of nodes as the Breadth-First method, only in the different order.

As the nodes on the single path are stored in each iteration from root to leaf node, the space requirement to store nodes is linear. With branching factor b and depth as m, the storage space is bm.

Disadvantage:

This algorithm may not terminate and go on infinitely on one path. The solution to this issue is to choose a cut-off depth. If the ideal cut-off is d, and if chosen cut-off is lesser than d, then this algorithm may fail. If chosen cut-off is more than d, then execution time increases.

Its complexity depends on the number of paths. It cannot check duplicate nodes.

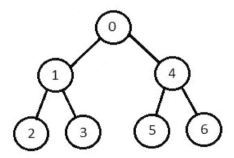

Bidirectional Search

It searches forward from an initial state and backward from goal state until both meets to identify a common state.

The path from the initial state is concatenated with the inverse path from the goal state. Each search is done only up to half of the total path.

Uniform Cost Search

Sorting is done in increasing the cost of the path to a node. It always expands the least cost node.

It is identical to Breadth-First search if each transition has the same cost.

It explores paths in the increasing order of cost.

Disadvantage:

There can be multiple long paths with the cost $\leq$ C*. Uniform Cost search must explore them all.

Iterative Deepening Depth-First Search

It performs a depth-first search to level 1, starts over, executes a complete depth-first search to level 2, and continues in such way till the solution is found.

It never creates a node until all lower nodes are generated. It only saves a stack of nodes. The algorithm ends when it finds a solution at depth d. The number of nodes created at depth d is bd and at depth d-1 is bd-1.

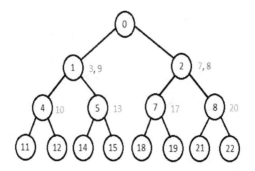

Comparison of Various Algorithms Complexities

Let us see the performance of algorithms based on various criteria:

Criterion	Breadth First	Depth First	Bidirectional	Uniform Cost	Iterative Deepening
Time	b^d	b^m	$b^{d/2}$	b^d	b^d
Space	b^d	b^m	$b^{d/2}$	b^d	b^d
Optimality	Y	N	Y	Y	Y
Completeness	Y	N	Y	Y	Y

Informed (Heuristic) Search Strategies

To solve large problems with a large number of possible states, problem-specific knowledge needs to be added to increase the efficiency of search algorithms.

Heuristic Evaluation Functions

They calculate the cost of an optimal path between two states. A heuristic function for sliding-tiles games is computed by counting a number of moves that each tile makes from its goal state and adding these number of moves for all tiles.

Pure Heuristic Search

It expands nodes in the order of their heuristic values. It creates two lists, a closed list for the already expanded nodes and an open list for the created but unexpanded nodes.

In each iteration, a node with a minimum heuristic value is expanded, all its child nodes are created and placed in the closed list. Then, the heuristic function is applied to the child nodes and they are placed in the open list according to their heuristic value. The shorter paths are saved and the longer ones are disposed of.

A* Search

It is the best-known form of Best First search. It avoids expanding paths that are already expensive, but expands most promising paths first.

$f(n) = g(n) + h(n)$, where

- $g(n)$ the cost (so far) to reach the node

- $h(n)$ estimated cost to get from the node to the goal

- $f(n)$ estimated total cost of path through n to goal. It is implemented using priority queue by increasing $f(n)$.

Greedy Best First Search

It expands the node that is estimated to be closest to goal. It expands nodes based on f(n) = h(n). It is implemented using priority queue.

Disadvantage: It can get stuck in loops. It is not optimal.

Local Search Algorithms

They start from a prospective solution and then move to a neighbouring solution. They can return a valid solution even if it is interrupted at any time before the end.

Hill-Climbing Search

It is an iterative algorithm that starts with an arbitrary solution to a problem and attempts to find a better solution by changing a single element of the solution incrementally. If the change produces a better solution, an incremental change is taken as a new solution. This process is repeated until there are no further improvements.

function Hill-Climbing (problem), returns a state that is a local maximum.

inputs: problem, a problem

local variables: current, a node

neighbour, a node

current ←Make_Node(Initial-State[problem])

loop

do neighbour ← a highest_valued successor of the current

if Value[neighbor] ≤ Value[current] then

return State[current]

current ← neighbour

end

Disadvantage: This algorithm is neither complete nor optimal.

Local Beam Search

In this algorithm, it holds k number of states at any given time. At the start, these states are generated randomly. The successors of these k states are computed with the help of objective function. If any of these successors is the maximum value of the objective function, then the algorithm stops.

Otherwise, the (initial k states and k number of successors of the states = 2k) states are placed in a pool. The pool is then sorted numerically. The highest k states are selected as new initial states. This process continues until a maximum value is reached.

function BeamSearch(problem, k), returns a solution state.

start with k randomly generated states

loop

generate all successors of all k states

if any of the states = solution, then return the state

else select the k best successors end

Simulated Annealing

Annealing is the process of heating and cooling metal to change its internal structure for modifying its physical properties. When the metal cools, its new structure is seized, and the metal retains its newly obtained properties. In the simulated annealing process, the temperature is kept variable.

We initially set the temperature high and then allow it to 'cool' slowly as the algorithm proceeds. When the temperature is high, the algorithm is allowed to accept worse solutions with high frequency.

Start

1. Initialize k = 0; L = integer number of variables;

2. From i -> j, search the performance difference Δ.

3. If Δ </T(k))Δ= 0 then accept else if exp(- > random(0,1) then accept;

4. Repeat steps 1 and 2 for L(k) steps.

5. k = k + 1;

Repeat steps 1 through 4 until the criteria is met.

End

Travelling Salesman Problem

In this algorithm, the objective is to find a low-cost tour that starts from a city, visits all cities en-route exactly once and ends at the same starting city.

Start

Find out all (n -1)! Possible solutions, where n is the total number of cities.

Determine the minimum cost by finding out the cost of each of these (n -1)!

solutions.

Finally, keep the one with the minimum cost.

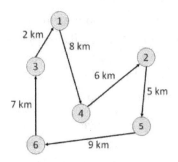

Total Distance = 37km

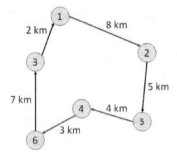

Total Distance = 31km

FUZZY LOGIC SYSTEMS

Fuzzy Logic Systems (FLS) produce acceptable but definite output in response to incomplete, ambiguous, distorted, or inaccurate (fuzzy) input.

What is Fuzzy Logic?

Fuzzy Logic (FL) is a method of reasoning that resembles human reasoning. The approach of FL imitates the way of decision making in humans that involves all intermediate possibilities between digital values YES and NO.

The conventional logic block that a computer can understand takes precise input and produces a definite output as TRUE or FALSE, which is equivalent to human's YES or NO.

The inventor of fuzzy logic, Lotfi Zadeh, observed that unlike computers, human decision making includes a range of possibilities between YES and NO, such as:

| CERTAINLY YES |
| POSSIBLY YES |
| CANNOT SAY |
| POSSIBLY NO |
| CERTAINLY NO |

1. Fuzzy Logic in Artificial Intelligence

In this Fuzzy Logic Tutorial, we will learn What is Fuzzy Logic Systems in Artificial Intelligence. Moreover, we will discuss the Application and Architecture of Fuzzy Logic in AI.

Along with this, we will learn why Fuzzy logic is used and what are its pros and cons.

So, let's start our journey of Fuzzy Logic System in AI.

2. Introduction to Fuzzy Logic in AI

a. What is Fuzzy Logic System?

Generally, it's a method of reasoning. Although, resembles human reasoning. Also, it has an approach to decision making in humans. As they involve all intermediate possibilities between digital values YES and NO.

Fuzzy Logic System was invented by Lotfi Zadeh. Also, he observed, unlike other computers, it includes a range of possibilities between YES and NO, in a human decision.

b. Implementation of Fuzzy Logic System

Basically, it can be implemented in systems with various sizes and capabilities. That should be range from mall micro-controllers to large. Also, it can be implemented in hardware, software, or a combination of both in artificial intelligence.

3. Why Fuzzy Logic?

Generally, we use the fuzzy logic system for the practical as well as commercial purposes.

We can use it to consumer products and control machines.

Although, not give accurate reasoning, but acceptable reasoning.

Also, this logic helps to deal with the uncertainty in engineering.

5. Fuzzy Logic Systems Architecture

Basically, four parts are shown in the architecture of the fuzzy logic system-

a. Fuzzification Module

We use this module to transform the system inputs. Also, helps in splitting the input signal into various five steps.

LP – x is Large Positive.

MP- x is Medium Positive.

S – x is Small.

MN – x is Medium Negative.

LN – x is Large Negative

b. Knowledge Base

In this, we have to store it in IF-THEN rules that were provided by experts.

c. Inference Engine

Generally, it helps in stimulating the human reasoning process. That is by making fuzzy inference on the inputs and IF-THEN rules.

d. Defuzzification Module

In this module, we have to transform the fuzzy set into a crisp value. That set was obtained by an inference engine. Although, the membership functions always work on the same concept i.e fuzzy sets of variables.

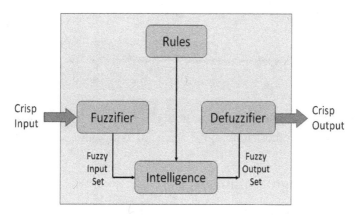

6. Membership Function

As this function allows you to quantify linguistic term. Also, represent a fuzzy set graphically. Although, MF for a fuzzy set A on the universe of discourse. That X is defined as $\mu A:X \rightarrow [0,1]$.

In this function, between a value of 0 and 1, each element of X is mapped. We can define it as the degree of membership. Also, it quantifies the degree of membership of the element. That is in X to the fuzzy set A.

- x-axis– It represents the universe of discourse.

- y-axis – It represents the degrees of membership in the [0, 1] interval.

We can apply different membership functions to fuzzify a numerical value. Also, we use simple functions as complex. As they do not add more precision in the output.

We can define all membership functions for LP, MP, S, MN, and LN. That is shown as below –

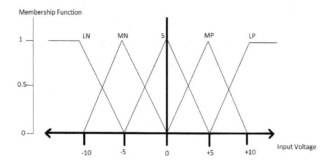

There is some common triangular membership function as compared to other functions. Such as singleton, Gaussian. And trapezoidal.

7. Fuzzy Logic Applications

There are some areas of a fuzzy logic system. These are-

a. Automotive Systems

Automatic Gearboxes

Four-Wheel Steering

Vehicle environment control

b. Consumer Electronic Goods

Hi-Fi Systems

Photocopiers

Still and Video Cameras

Television

c. Domestic Goods

Microwave Ovens

Refrigerators

Toasters

Vacuum Cleaners

Washing Machines

d. Environment Control

Air Conditioners/Dryers/Heaters

Humidifiers

8. Advantages of Fuzzy Logic Systems

Generally, in this system, we can take imprecise, distorted, noisy input information.

Also, these logics are easy to construct and understand.

Basically, it's a solution to complex problems. Such as medicine.

Also, we can relate math in concept within fuzzy logic. Also, these concepts are very simple.

Due to the flexibility of fuzzy logic, we can add and delete rules in the FLS system.

9. Disadvantages of Fuzzy Logic Systems

Till no designing approach to this fuzzy logic.

Basically, if logics are simple, then one can understand it.

Also, suitable for problems which do not have high accuracy.

So, this was all about Fuzzy Logic systems in AI. Hope you like our explanation.

10. Conclusion

As a result, we have studied Fuzzy Logic systems in AI. Also, implementation, need etc. As this will help you to understand in a better manner with the help of images. Furthermore, if you feel any query, feel free to ask in the comment section.

Example of a Fuzzy Logic System

Let us consider an air conditioning system with a 5-level fuzzy logic system. This system adjusts the temperature of the air conditioner by comparing the room temperature and the target temperature value.

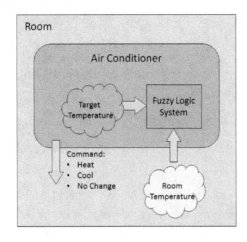

Algorithm

2 Define linguistic Variables and terms (start)

3 Construct membership functions for them. (start)

4 Construct a knowledge base of rules (start)

5 Convert crisp data into fuzzy data sets using membership functions (fuzzification)

6 Evaluate rules in the rule base (inference engine)

7 Combine results from each rule (inference engine)

8 Convert output data into non-fuzzy values. (defuzzification)

Development

Step 1:

Define linguistic variables and terms

Linguistic variables are input and output variables in the form of simple words or sentences.

For room temperature, cold, warm, hot, etc., are linguistic terms.

Temperature (t) = {very-cold, cold, warm, very-warm, hot}

Every member of this set is a linguistic term and it can cover some portion of overall temperature values.

Step 2:

Construct membership functions for them

The membership functions of the temperature variable are as shown:

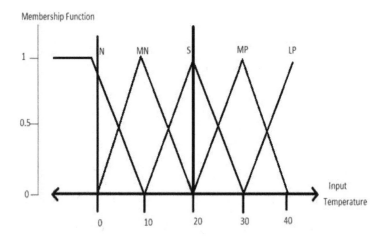

Step3:

Construct knowledge base rules

Create a matrix of room temperature values versus target temperature values that an air conditioning system is expected to provide.

RoomTemp/Target	Very_Cold	Cold	Warm	Hot	Very_Hot
Very_Cold	No Change	Heat	Heat	Heat	Heat
Cold	Cool	No Change	Heat	Heat	Heat
Warm	Cool	Cool	No Change	Heat	Heat
Hot	Cool	Cool	Cool	No Change	Heat

Very_Hot	Cool	Cool	Cool	Cool	No Change

Build a set of rules into the knowledge base in the form of IF-THEN-ELSE structures.

Sr. No.	Condition	Action
1	IF temperature=(Cold OR Very_Cold) AND target=Warm THEN	HEAT
2	IF temperature=(Hot OR Very_Hot) AND target=Warm THEN	COOL
3	IF (temperature=Warm) AND (target=Warm) THEN	NOCHANGE

Step5

Fuzzy set operations perform the evaluation of rules. The operations used for OR and AND are Max and Min respectively. All results of the evaluation are combined to form a final result. This result is a fuzzy value.

Step 6

Defuzzification is then performed according to the membership function for the output variable.

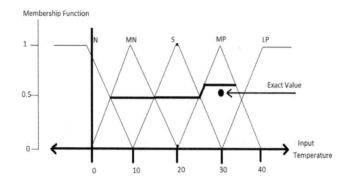

Application Areas of Fuzzy Logic

The key application areas of fuzzy logic are as given:

Automotive Systems

- Automatic Gearboxes
- Four-Wheel Steering
- Vehicle environment control

Consumer Electronics

- Hi-Fi Systems
- Photocopiers
- Still and Video Cameras
- Television

Domestic Goods

- Microwave Ovens
- Refrigerators
- Toasters
- Vacuum Cleaners
  - Washing Machines

Environment Control

- Air Conditioners/Dryers/Heaters
- Humidifiers

Advantages of FLSs

- Mathematical concepts within fuzzy reasoning are very simple.
- You can modify a FIS by just adding or deleting rules due to flexibility of fuzzy logic.
- Fuzzy logic Systems can take imprecise, distorted, noisy input information.
- FLSs are easy to construct and understand.
- Fuzzy logic is a solution to complex problems in all fields of life, including medicine, as it resembles human reasoning and decision making.

Disadvantages of FLSs

- There is no systematic approach to fuzzy system designing.
- They are understandable only when simple.

  They are suitable for problems which do not need high accuracy.

NATURAL LANGUAGE PROCESSING

Natural Language Processing (NLP) refers to the AI method of communicating with an intelligent system using a natural language such as English.

Processing of Natural Language is required when you want an intelligent system like a robot to perform as per your instructions, when you want to hear a decision from a dialogue based clinical expert system, etc.

The field of NLP involves making computers to perform useful tasks with the natural languages humans use. The input and output of an NLP system can be:

- Speech
- Written Text

Components of NLP

There are two components of NLP as given:

Natural Language Understanding (NLU)

Understanding involves the following tasks:

- Mapping the given input in natural language into useful representations.
- Analyzing different aspects of the language.

Natural Language Generation (NLG)

It is the process of producing meaningful phrases and sentences in the form of natural language from some internal representation.

It involves:

- Text planning: It includes retrieving the relevant content from the knowledge base.

- Sentence planning: It includes choosing the required words, forming meaningful phrases, setting the tone of the sentence.

- Text Realization: It is mapping sentence plan into sentence structure.

The NLU is harder than NLG.

Difficulties in NLU

NL has an extremely rich form and structure.

It is very ambiguous. There can be different levels of ambiguity:

- Lexical ambiguity: It is at a very primitive level such as word-level.

- For example, treating the word "board" as a noun or a verb?

- Syntax Level ambiguity: A sentence can be parsed in different ways.

- For example, "He lifted the beetle with a red cap." – Did he use the cap to lift the beetle or he lifted a beetle that had a red cap?

- Referential ambiguity: Referring to something using pronouns. For example, Rima went to Gauri. She said, "I am tired." - Exactly who is tired?

- One input can mean different meanings. o Many inputs can mean the same thing.

NLP Terminology

- Phonology: It is the study of organizing sound systematically.

- Morphology: It is a study of the construction of words from primitive meaningful units.

- Morpheme: It is a primitive unit of meaning in a language.

- Syntax: It refers to arranging words to make a sentence. It also involves determining the structural role of words in the sentence and in phrases.

- Semantics: It is concerned with the meaning of words and how to combine words into meaningful phrases and sentences.

- Pragmatics: It deals with using and understanding sentences in different situations and how the interpretation of the sentence is affected.

- Discourse: It deals with how the immediately preceding sentence can affect the interpretation of the next sentence.

- World Knowledge: It includes general knowledge about the world.

Steps in NLP

There are generally five steps:

1. Lexical Analysis

It involves identifying and analyzing the structure of words. Lexicon of a language means the collection of words and phrases in a language. Lexical analysis is dividing the whole chunk of text into paragraphs, sentences, and words.

2. Syntactic Analysis (Parsing)

It involves the analysis of words in the sentence for grammar and arranging words in a manner that shows the relationship among the words. The sentence such as "The school goes to boy" is rejected by English syntactic analyzer.

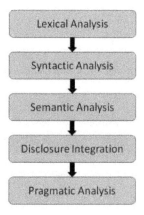

3. Semantic Analysis

It draws the exact meaning or the dictionary meaning from the text. The text is checked for meaningfulness. It is done by mapping syntactic structures and objects in the task domain. The semantic analyzer disregards sentence such as "hot ice-cream".

4. Discourse Integration

The meaning of any sentence depends upon the meaning of the sentence just before it. In addition, it also brings about the meaning of immediately succeeding sentence.

5. Pragmatic Analysis

During this, what was said is re-interpreted on what it actually meant. It involves deriving those aspects of language which require real-world knowledge.

Implementation Aspects of Syntactic Analysis

There are a number of algorithms researchers have developed for syntactic analysis, but we consider only the following simple methods:

- Context-Free Grammar

- Top-Down Parser

Let us see them in detail:

Context-Free Grammar

It is the grammar that consists of rules with a single symbol on the left-hand side of the rewrite rules. Let us create a grammar to parse a sentence –

"The bird pecks the grains"

Articles (DET): a | an | the.

Nouns: bird | birds | grain | grains

Noun Phrase (NP): Article + Noun | Article + Adjective + Noun

= DET N | DET ADJ N

Verbs: pecks | pecking | pecked

Verb Phrase (VP): NP V | V NP

Adjectives (ADJ): beautiful | small | chirping

The parse tree breaks down the sentence into structured parts so that the computer can easily understand and process it. In order for the parsing algorithm to construct this parse tree, a set of rewrite rules, which describe what tree structures are legal, need to be constructed.

These rules say that a certain symbol may be expanded in the tree by a sequence of other symbols. According to first-order logic rule, ff there are two strings Noun Phrase (NP) and Verb Phrase (VP), then the string combined by NP followed by VP is a sentence. The rewrite rules for the sentence are as follows:

S -> NP VP

NP -> DET N | DET ADJ N

VP -> V NP

Lexocon:

DET -> a | the

ADJ -> beautiful | perching

N -> bird | birds | grain | grains

V -> peck | pecks | pecking

The parse tree can be created as shown:

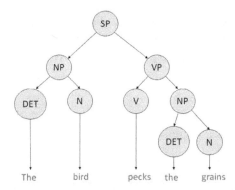

Now consider the above rewrite rules. Since V can be replaced by both, "peck" or "pecks", sentences such as "The bird peck the grains" can be wrongly permitted. i. e. the subject-verb agreement error is approved as correct.

Merit:

The simplest style of grammar, therefore widely used one.

Demerits:

- They are not highly precise. For example, "The grains peck the bird", is a syntactically correct according to parser, but even if it makes no sense, parser takes it as a correct sentence.

- To bring out high precision, multiple sets of grammar need to be prepared. It may require a completely different set of rules for parsing singular and plural variations, passive sentences, etc., which can lead to the creation of a huge set of rules that are unmanageable.

Top-Down Parser

Here, the parser starts with the S symbol and attempts to rewrite it into a sequence

of terminal symbols that match the classes of the words in the input sentence until it consists entirely of terminal symbols.

These are then checked with the input sentence to see if it matched. If not, the process is started over again with a different set of rules. This is repeated until a specific rule is found which describes the structure of the sentence.

Merit:

It is simple to implement.

Demerits:

- It is inefficient, as the search process has to be repeated if an error occurs.

- Slow speed of working.

ROBOTICS

Robotics is a domain in artificial intelligence that deals with the study of creating intelligent and efficient robots.

What are Robots?

Robots are the artificial agents acting in a real-world environment.

Objective

Robots are aimed at manipulating the objects by perceiving, picking, moving, modifying the physical properties of objects, destroying it, or to have an effect thereby freeing manpower from doing repetitive functions without getting bored, distracted, or exhausted.

What is Robotics?

Robotics is a branch of AI, which is composed of Electrical Engineering, Mechanical Engineering, and Computer Science for designing, construction, and application of robots.

Robotics is a scientific and engineering discipline that is focused on the understanding and use of artificial, embodied capabilities. The people who work in this field (roboticists) come from mechanical engineering, electronic engineering, information engineering, computer science, and other fields. On the engineering side, roboticists deal with the design, construction, operation, and use of robots, especially through computer systems for their control, sensory feedback, and information processing. On the scientific side, roboticists study how a robot's environment and design affect how well it does its job.

Robots are machines that can substitute for humans and replicate human actions and are used to do jobs that are difficult, impossible, or just tedious for humans to do. Robots can be used in many situations and for lots of purposes, but today many are used in dangerous environments (including bomb detection and deactivation), manufacturing processes, or where humans cannot survive (e.g. in space, underwater, in high heat, and for clean up and containment of hazardous materials and radiation). Robots can take on any form but some are made to resemble humans in appearance. This is said to help in the acceptance of a robot in certain replicative behaviours usually performed by people. Such robots attempt to replicate walking, lifting, speech, cognition, or any other human activity. Many of today's robots are inspired by nature, contributing to the field of bio-inspired robotics.

The concept of creating machines that can operate autonomously dates back to classical times, but research into the functionality and potential uses of robots did not grow substantially until the 20th century. Throughout history, it has been frequently assumed by various scholars, inventors, engineers, and technicians that robots will one day be able to mimic human behaviour and manage tasks in a human-like fashion. Today, robotics is a rapidly growing field, as technological advances continue; researching, designing, and building new robots serve various practical purposes, whether domestically, commercially, or militarily. Many robots are built to do jobs that are hazardous to people, such as defusing bombs, finding survivors in unstable ruins, and exploring mines and shipwrecks. Robotics is also used in STEM (science, technology, engineering, and mathematics) as a teaching aid. The advent of nanorobots, microscopic robots that can be injected into the human body, could revolutionize medicine and human health.

Robotics has historically been considered a branch of engineering that involves the conception, design, manufacture, and operation of robots. This field overlaps with electronics, computer science, artificial intelligence, mechatronics, nanotechnology and bioengineering.

Robotic aspects

There are many types of robots; they are used in many different environments and for many different uses, although being very diverse in application and form they all share three basic similarities when it comes to their construction:

Robots all have some kind of mechanical construction, a frame, form or shape designed to achieve a particular task. For example, a robot designed to travel across heavy dirt or mud, might use caterpillar tracks. The mechanical aspect is mostly the creator's solution to completing the assigned task and dealing with the physics of the environment around it. Form follows function.

Robots have electrical components which power and control the machinery. For example, the robot with caterpillar tracks would need some kind of power to move the tracker treads. That power comes in the form of electricity, which will have to travel through a wire and originate from a battery, a basic electrical circuit. Even petrol powered machines that get their power mainly from petrol still require an electric current to start the combustion process which is why most petrol-powered machines like cars, have batteries. The electrical aspect of robots is used for movement (through motors), sensing (where electrical signals are used to measure things like heat, sound, position, and energy status) and operation (robots need some level of electrical energy supplied to their motors and sensors in order to activate and perform basic operations) All robots contain some level of computer programming code. A program is how a robot decides when or how to do something. In the caterpillar track example, a robot that needs to move across a muddy road may have the correct mechanical construction and receive the correct amount of power from its battery, but would not go anywhere without a program telling it to move. Programs are the core essence of a robot, it could have excellent mechanical and electrical construction, but if its program is poorly constructed its performance will be very poor (or it may not perform at all). There are three different types of robotic programs: remote control, artificial intelligence and hybrid. A robot with remote control programing has a preexisting set of commands that it will only perform if and when it receives a signal from a control source, typically a human being with a remote control. It is perhaps more appropriate to view devices controlled primarily by human commands as falling in the discipline of automation rather than robotics. Robots that use artificial intelligence interact with their environment on their own without a control source, and can determine reactions to objects and problems they encounter using their preexisting programming. Hybrid is a form of programming that incorporates both AI and RC functions.

The difference in Robot System and Other AI Program

Here is the difference between the two:

AI Programs	Robots
They usually operate in computer-simulated worlds.	They operate in the real physical world
The input to an AI program is in symbols and rules.	Inputs to robots are analog signal in the form of speech waveform or images
They need general-purpose computers to operate on.	They need special hardware with sensors and effectors.

Robot Locomotion

Locomotion is the mechanism that makes a robot capable of moving in its environment. Robot locomotion is the collective name for the various methods that robots use to transport themselves from place to place.

Wheeled robots are typically quite energy efficient and simple to control. However, other forms of locomotion may be more appropriate for a number of reasons, for example traversing rough terrain, as well as moving and interacting in human environments. Furthermore, studying bipedal and insect-like robots may beneficially impact on biomechanics.

A major goal in this field is in developing capabilities for robots to autonomously decide how, when, and where to move. However, coordinating numerous robot joints for even simple matters, like negotiating stairs, is difficult. Autonomous robot locomotion is a major technological obstacle for many areas of robotics, such as humanoids.

There are various types of locomotions:

- Legged
- Wheeled
- Combination of Legged and Wheeled Locomotion
- Tracked slip/skid

Legged Locomotion

Legged robots can traverse on challenging terrain, to use perception to plan for footstep locations and to navigate in the environment, as well as to execute manipulation tasks. A legged system is an omnidirectional platform which can negotiate obstacles with a comparable size of the robot. Such unique mobility capabilities make these platforms a perfect candidate for scenarios such as search and rescue, inspection, and exploration tasks, which typically require machines capable of traversing challenging terrain and negotiating obstacles.

- This type of locomotion consumes more power while demonstrating walk, jump, trot, hop, climb up or down, etc.

- It requires more number of motors to accomplish a movement. It is suited for rough as well as smooth terrain where irregular or too smooth surface makes it consume more power for a wheeled locomotion. It is a little difficult to implement because of stability issues.

- It comes with the variety of one, two, four, and six legs. If a robot has multiple legs then leg coordination is necessary for locomotion.

The total number of possible gaits (a periodic sequence of lift and release events for each of the total legs) a robot can travel depends upon the number of its legs.

If a robot has k legs, then the number of possible events N = (2k-1)!.

In the case of a two-legged robot (k=2), the number of possible events is N = (2k-1)!

$$= (2*2-1)! = 3! = 6.$$

Hence there are six possible different events:

1 Lifting the Left leg

2 Releasing the Left leg

3 Lifting the Right leg

4 Releasing the Right leg

5 Lifting both the legs together

6 Releasing both the legs together.

In the case of k=6 legs, there are 39916800 possible events. Hence the complexity of robots is directly proportional to the number of legs.

A walking robot generates its motion by producing reaction forces between its legs and the terrain on which it is locomoting. Due to the hybrid nature of this platform, several challenges specific to legged locomotion arise when implementing the set of skills necessary to navigate in a real-world environment. One of the essential characteristics of a successful motion control structure is how fast it can recompute its solution. In Robotic System Lab, we use optimization-based methods for both motion tracking and motion planning.

Wheeled Locomotion

Wheeled motion is the most popular locomotion mechanism in robotics. This mechanism enables a robot to move rapidly and requires less energy when compared to other types of robotic locomotion mechanisms. In addition, the wheeled mechanism is easy to control due to its good stability and the simplicity of the mechanism.

There are different variations of wheeled robots. In general, these robots are less resistant to derailing and consume less power while using narrow wheels. Large wheels with a rough surface pattern, on the other hand, are well-suited for uneven or soft ground surfaces.

It requires fewer number of motors to accomplish a movement. It is little easy to implement as there are less stability issues in case of more number of wheels. It is power efficient as compared to legged locomotion.

- Standard wheel: Rotates around the wheel axle and around the contact

- Castor wheel: Rotates around the wheel axle and the offset steering joint

- Swedish 45° and Swedish 90° wheels: Omni-wheel, rotates around the contact point, around the wheel axle, and around the rollers.

- Ball or spherical wheel: Omnidirectional wheel, technically difficult to implement.

Slip/Skid Locomotion

In this type, the vehicles use tracks as in a tank. The robot is steered by moving the tracks with different speeds in the same or opposite direction. It offers stability because of the large contact area of track and ground.

Components of a Robot

Power source

At present, mostly (lead-acid) batteries are used as a power source. Many different types of batteries can be used as a power source for robots. They range from lead-acid batteries, which are safe and have relatively long shelf lives but are rather heavy compared to silver–cadmium batteries that are much smaller in volume and are currently much more expensive. Designing a battery-powered robot needs to take into account factors such as safety, cycle lifetime and weight. Generators, often some type of internal combustion engine, can also be used. However, such designs are often mechanically complex and need fuel, require heat dissipation and are relatively heavy. A tether connecting the robot to a power supply would remove the power supply from the robot entirely. This has the advantage of saving weight and space by moving all power generation and storage components elsewhere. However, this design does come with the drawback of constantly having a cable connected to the robot, which can be difficult to manage. Potential power sources could be:

- pneumatic (compressed gases)

- Solar power (using the sun's energy and converting it into electrical power)

- hydraulics (liquids)

- flywheel energy storage

- organic garbage (through anaerobic digestion)

- nuclear

Actuation

Actuators are the "muscles" of a robot, the parts which convert stored energy into movement. By far the most popular actuators are electric motors that rotate a wheel or gear, and linear actuators that control industrial robots in factories. There are some recent advances in alternative types of actuators, powered by electricity, chemicals, or compressed air.

Electric motors

The vast majority of robots use electric motors, often brushed and brushless DC motors in portable robots or AC motors in industrial robots and computer numerical control machines. These motors are often preferred in systems with lighter loads, and where the predominant form of motion is rotational.

Linear actuators

Various types of linear actuators move in and out instead of by spinning, and often have quicker direction changes, particularly when very large forces are needed such as with industrial robotics. They are typically powered by compressed and oxidized air (pneumatic actuator) or an oil (hydraulic actuator) Linear actuators can also be powered by electricity which usually consists of a motor and a leadscrew. Another common type is a mechanical linear actuator that is turned by hand, such as a rack and pinion on a car.

Series elastic actuators

A flexure is designed as part of the motor actuator, to improve safety and provide robust force control, energy efficiency, shock absorption (mechanical filtering) while reducing excessive wear on the transmission and other mechanical components. The resultant lower reflected inertia can improve safety when a robot is interacting with humans or during collisions. It has been used in various robots, particularly advanced manufacturing robots and walking humanoid robots.

Air muscles

Pneumatic artificial muscles, also known as air muscles, are special tubes that expand (typically up to 40%) when air is forced inside them. They are used in some robot applications.

Muscle wire

Muscle wire, also known as shape memory alloy, Nitinol® or Flexinol® wire, is a material which contracts (under 5%) when electricity is applied. They have been used for some small robot applications.

Electroactive polymers

EAPs or EPAMs are plastic materials that can contract substantially (up to 380% activation strain) from electricity and have been used in facial muscles and arms of humanoid robots, and to enable new robots to float, fly, swim or walk.

Piezo motors

Recent alternatives to DC motors are piezo motors or ultrasonic motors. These work on a fundamentally different principle, whereby tiny piezoceramic elements, vibrating many thousands of times per second, cause linear or rotary motion. There are different mechanisms of operation; one type uses the vibration of the piezo elements to step the motor in a circle or a straight line. Another type uses the piezo elements to cause a nut to vibrate or to drive a screw. The advantages of these motors are nanometer resolution, speed, and available force for their size. These motors are already available commercially, and being used on some robots.

Elastic nanotubes

Elastic nanotubes are a promising artificial muscle technology in early-stage experimental development. The absence of defects in carbon nanotubes enables these filaments to deform elastically by several percent, with energy storage levels of perhaps 10 J/cm3 for metal nanotubes. Human biceps could be replaced with an 8 mm diameter wire of this material. Such compact "muscle" might allow future robots to outrun and outjump humans.

Sensing

Sensors allow robots to receive information about a certain measurement of the environment, or internal components. This is essential for robots to perform their tasks, and act upon any changes in the environment to calculate the appropriate response. They are used for various forms of measurements, to give the robots warnings about safety or malfunctions, and to provide real-time information of the task it is performing.

Touch

Current robotic and prosthetic hands receive far less tactile information than the human hand. Recent research has developed a tactile sensor array that mimics the mechanical properties and touches receptors of human fingertips. The sensor array is constructed as a rigid core surrounded by conductive fluid contained by an elastomeric skin. Electrodes are mounted on the surface of the rigid core and are connected to an impedance-measuring device within the core. When the artificial skin touches an object the fluid path around the electrodes is deformed, producing impedance changes that map the forces received from the object. The researchers expect that an important function of such artificial fingertips will be adjusting robotic grip on held objects.

Scientists from several European countries and Israel developed a prosthetic hand in 2009, called SmartHand, which functions like a real one—allowing patients to write with it, type on a keyboard, play piano and perform other fine movements. The prosthesis has sensors which enable the patient to sense real feeling in its fingertips.

Vision

Computer vision is the science and technology of machines that see. As a scientific discipline, computer vision is concerned with the theory behind artificial systems that extract information from images. The image data can take many forms, such as video sequences and views from cameras.

In most practical computer vision applications, the computers are pre-programmed to solve a particular task, but methods based on learning are now becoming increasingly common.

Computer vision systems rely on image sensors which detect electromagnetic radiation which is typically in the form of either visible light or infra-red light. The sensors are designed using solid-state physics. The process by which light propagates and reflects off surfaces is explained using optics. Sophisticated image sensors even require quantum mechanics to provide a complete understanding of the image formation process. Robots can also be equipped with multiple vision sensors to be better able to compute the sense of depth in the environment. Like human eyes, robots' "eyes" must also be able to focus on a particular area of interest, and also adjust to variations in light intensities.

There is a subfield within computer vision where artificial systems are designed to mimic the processing and behaviour of a biological system, at different levels of complexity. Also, some of the learning-based methods developed within computer vision have their background in biology.

In a short summary, Robots are constructed with the following:

- Power Supply: The robots are powered by batteries, solar power, hydraulic, or pneumatic power sources.

- Actuators: They convert energy into movement.

- Electric motors (AC/DC): They are required for rotational movement.

- Pneumatic Air Muscles: They contract almost 40% when air is sucked in them.

- Muscle Wires: They contract by 5% when an electric current is passed through them.

- Piezo Motors and Ultrasonic Motors: Best for industrial robots.

- Sensors: They provide knowledge of real-time information on the task environment. Robots are equipped with vision sensors to be to compute the depth in the environment. A tactile sensor imitates the mechanical properties of touch receptors of human fingertips.

Computer Vision

This is a technology of AI with which the robots can see. The computer vision plays a vital role in the domains of safety, security, health, access, and entertainment.

Computer vision automatically extracts, analyzes, and comprehends useful information from a single image or an array of images. This process involves the development of algorithms to accomplish automatic visual comprehension.

The hardware of Computer Vision System

This involves:

- Power supply

- Image acquisition device such as camera

- A processor

- A software
- A display device for monitoring the system
- Accessories such as camera stands, cables, and connectors

Tasks of Computer Vision

OCR: In the domain of computers, Optical Character Reader, a software to convert scanned documents into editable text, which accompanies a scanner.

Face Detection: Many state-of-the-art cameras come with this feature, which enables to read the face and take the picture of that perfect expression. It is used to let a user access the software on the correct match.

Object Recognition: They are installed in supermarkets, cameras, high-end cars such as BMW, GM, and Volvo.

Estimating Position: It is estimating the position of an object with respect to the camera as in the position of the tumour in the human body.

Application Domains of Computer Vision

- agriculture
- autonomous vehicles
- biometrics
- character recognition
- forensics, security, and surveillance
- industrial quality inspection
- face recognition
- gesture analysis
- geoscience
- medical imagery
- pollution monitoring

- process control

- remote sensing

- robotics

- transport

Applications of Robotics

As more and more robots are designed for specific tasks this method of classification becomes more relevant. For example, many robots are designed for assembly work, which may not be readily adaptable for other applications. They are termed as "assembly robots". For seam welding, some suppliers provide complete welding systems with the robot i.e. the welding equipment along with other material handling facilities like turntables, etc. as an integrated unit. Such an integrated robotic system is called a "welding robot" even though its discrete manipulator unit could be adapted to a variety of tasks. Some robots are specifically designed for heavy load manipulation, and are labelled as "heavy-duty robots".

The robotics has been instrumental in the various domains such as:

- **Industries:** Robots are used for handling material, cutting, welding, colour coating, drilling, polishing, etc.

- **Military:** Autonomous robots can reach inaccessible and hazardous zones during war. A robot named Daksh, developed by Defense Research and Development Organization (DRDO), is in function to destroy life-threatening objects safely.

- **Medicine:** The robots are capable of carrying out hundreds of clinical tests simultaneously, rehabilitating permanently disabled people, and performing complex surgeries such as brain tumours.

- **Exploration:** The robot rock climbers used for space exploration, underwater drones used for ocean exploration are to name a few.

  Entertainment: Disney's engineers have created hundreds of robots for movie making.

NEURAL NETWORKS

Yet another research area in AI, neural networks, is inspired from the natural neural network of human nervous system.

What are Artificial Neural Networks (ANNs)?

Artificial Neural Networks are computing systems made up of a number of simple, highly interconnected processing elements, which process information by their dynamic state response to external inputs

Basic Structure of ANNs

The idea of ANNs is based on the belief that working of human brain by making the right connections, can be imitated using silicon and wires as living neurons and dendrites.

The human brain is composed of 100 billion nerve cells called neurons. They are connected to other thousand cells by Axons. Stimuli from the external environment or inputs from sensory organs are accepted by dendrites. These inputs create electric impulses, which quickly travel through the neural network. A neuron can then send the message to other neurons to handle the issue or does not send it forward.

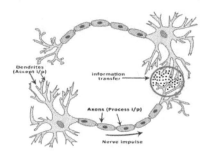

ANNs are composed of multiple nodes, which imitate biological neurons of the human brain. The neurons are connected by links and they interact with each other. The nodes can take input data and perform simple operations on the data. The result of these operations is passed to other neurons. The output at each node is called its activation or node value.

Each link is associated with weight. ANNs are capable of learning, which takes place by altering weight values. The following illustration shows a simple ANN:

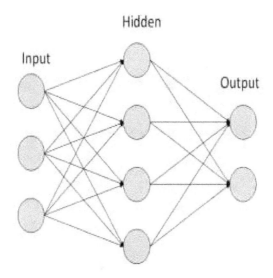

Types of Artificial Neural Networks

There are two Artificial Neural Network topologies: FeedForward and Feedback.

FeedForward ANN

In this ANN, the information flow is unidirectional. A unit sends information to other units from which it does not receive any information. There are no feedback loops. They are used in pattern generation/recognition/classification. They have fixed inputs and outputs.

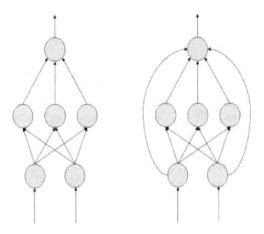

Feedback ANN

Here, feedback loops are allowed. They are used in content-addressable memories.

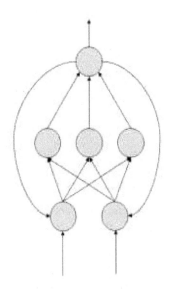

Working of ANNs

In the topology diagrams shown, each arrow represents a connection between two neurons and indicates the pathway for the flow of information. Each connection has a weight, an integer number that controls the signal between the two neurons.

If the network generates a "good or desired" output, there is no need to adjust the weights. However, if the network generates a "poor or undesired" output or an error, then the system alters the weights in order to improve subsequent results.

Machine Learning in ANNs

ANNs are capable of learning and they need to be trained. There are several learning strategies:

- Supervised Learning: It involves a teacher that is scholar than the ANN itself. For example, the teacher feeds some example data about which the teacher already knows the answers.

  For example, pattern recognizing. The ANN comes up with guesses while recognizing. Then the teacher provides the ANN with the answers. The network then compares it guesses with the teacher's "correct" answers and makes adjustments according to errors.

- Unsupervised Learning: It is required when there is no example data set with known answers. For example, searching for a hidden pattern. In this case, clustering i.e. dividing a set of elements into groups according to some unknown pattern is carried out based on the existing data sets present.

- Reinforcement Learning: This strategy built on observation. The ANN makes a decision by observing its environment. If the observation is negative, the network adjusts its weights to be able to make a different required decision the next time.

Back Propagation Algorithm

It is the training or learning algorithm. It learns by example. If you submit to the algorithm the example of what you want the network to do, it changes the network's weights so that it can produce desired output for a particular input on finishing the training.

Back Propagation networks are ideal for simple Pattern Recognition and Mapping Tasks.

Bayesian Networks (BN)

These are the graphical structures used to represent the probabilistic relationship among a set of random variables. Bayesian networks are also called Belief Networks or Bayes Nets. BNs reason about uncertain domain.

In these networks, each node represents a random variable with specific propositions. For example, in a medical diagnosis domain, the node Cancer represents the proposition that a patient has cancer.

The edges connecting the nodes represent probabilistic dependencies among those random variables. If out of two nodes, one is affecting the other then they must be directly connected in the directions of the effect. The strength of the relationship between variables is quantified by the probability associated with each node.

There is an only constraint on the arcs in a BN that you cannot return to a node simply by following directed arcs. Hence the BNs are called Directed Acyclic Graphs (DAGs).

BNs are capable of handling multivalued variables simultaneously. The BN variables are composed of two dimensions:

1. Range of prepositions

2. Probability assigned to each of the prepositions.

Consider a finite set $X = \{X1, X2, ...,Xn\}$ of discrete random variables, where each variable Xi may take values from a finite set, denoted by $Val(Xi)$. If there is a directed link from variable Xi to variable, Xj, then variable Xi will be a parent of variable Xj showing direct dependencies between the variables.

The structure of BN is ideal for combining prior knowledge and observed data. BN can be used to learn the causal relationships and understand various problem domains and to predict future events, even in case of missing data.

Building a Bayesian Network

A knowledge engineer can build a Bayesian network. There are a number of steps the knowledge engineer needs to take while building it.

Example problem: Lung cancer. A patient has been suffering from breathlessness. He visits the doctor, suspecting he has lung cancer. The doctor knows that barring lung cancer, there are various other possible diseases the patient might have such as tuberculosis and bronchitis.

Gather Relevant Information of Problem

- Is the patient a smoker? If yes, then high chances of cancer and bronchitis.

- Is the patient exposed to air pollution? If yes, what sort of air pollution?

- Take an X-Ray positive X-ray would indicate either TB or lung cancer.

Identify Interesting Variables

The knowledge engineer tries to answer the questions:

- Which nodes to represent?

- What values can they take? In which state can they be?

For now let us consider nodes, with only discrete values. The variable must take on exactly one of these values at a time.

Common types of discrete nodes are:

- Boolean nodes: They represent propositions, taking binary values TRUE (T) and FALSE (F).

- Ordered values: A node Pollution might represent and take values from {low, medium, high} describing the degree of a patient's exposure to pollution.

- Integral values: A node called Age might represent patient's age with possible values from 1 to 120. Even at this early stage, modelling choices are being made.

Create Arcs between Nodes

The topology of the network should capture qualitative relationships between variables.

For example, what causes a patient to have lung cancer? - Pollution and smoking. Then add arcs from node Pollution and node Smoker to node Lung-Cancer.

Similarly if the patient has lung cancer, then X-ray result will be positive. Then add arcs from Lung-Cancer to X-Ray.

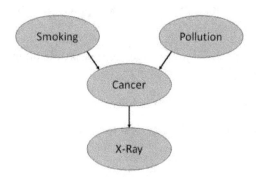

Specify Topology

Conventionally, BNs are laid out so that the arcs point from top to bottom. The set of parent nodes of a node X is given by Parents(X).

The Lung-Cancer node has two parents (reasons or causes): Pollution and Smoker, while node Smoker is an ancestor of node X-Ray. Similarly, X-Ray is a child (consequence or effects) of node Lung-Cancer and successor of nodes Smoker and Pollution.

Conditional Probabilities

Now quantify the relationships between connected nodes: this is done by specifying a conditional probability distribution for each node. As only discrete variables are considered here, this takes the form of a Conditional Probability Table (CPT).

First, for each node, we need to look at all the possible combinations of values of those parent nodes. Each such combination is called an instantiation of the parent set. For each distinct instantiation of parent node values, we need to specify the probability that the child will take.

For example, the Lung-Cancer node's parents are Pollution and Smoking. They take the possible values = { (H,T), (H,F), (L,T), (L,F)}. The CPT specifies the probability of cancer for each of these cases as <0.05, 0.02, 0.03, 0.001> respectively.

Applications of Neural Networks

They can perform tasks that are easy for a human but difficult for a machine:

- **Aerospace:** Autopilot aircrafts, aircraft fault detection.

- **Automotive:** Automobile guidance systems.

- **Military:** Weapon steering, target tracking, object discrimination, facial recognition, signal/image identification.

- **Electronics:** Code sequence prediction, IC chip layout, chip failure analysis, machine vision, voice synthesis.

- **Financial:** Real estate appraisal, loan advisor, mortgage screening, corporate bond rating, portfolio trading program, corporate financial analysis, currency value prediction, document readers, credit application evaluators.

- **Industrial:** Manufacturing process control, product design and analysis, quality inspection systems, welding quality analysis, paper quality prediction, chemical product design analysis, dynamic modelling of chemical process systems, machine maintenance analysis, project bidding, planning, and management.

- **Medical:** Cancer cell analysis, EEG and ECG analysis, prosthetic design, transplant time optimizer.

- **Speech:** Speech recognition, speech classification, text to speech conversion.

- **Telecommunications:** Image and data compression, automated information services, real-time spoken language translation.

- Transportation: Truck brake diagnosis, vehicle scheduling, routing systems.

- **Software:** Pattern Recognition in facial recognition, optical character recognition, etc.

- **Time Series Prediction:** ANNs are used to make predictions on stocks and natural calamities.

- **Signal Processing:** Neural networks can be trained to process an audio signal and filter it appropriately in the hearing aids.

- **Control:** ANNs are often used to make steering decisions of physical vehicles.

- **Anomaly Detection:** As ANNs are expert at recognizing patterns, they can also be trained to generate an output when something unusual occurs that misfits the pattern.

OUTLOOKS AND CONCLUSION

Artificial Intelligence is a concept that concerned people from all around the world and from all times. Ancient Greeks and Egyptians represented in their myths and philosophy machines and artificial entities which have qualities resembling to those of humans, especially in what thinking, reasoning and intelligence are concerned.

Artificial intelligence is a branch of computer science concerned with the study and the design of intelligent machines. The term "artificial intelligence", coined at the conference that took place at Dartmouth in 1956 comes from John McCarthy who defined it as the science of creating intelligent machine.

Along with the development of the electronic computers, back in the 1940s, this domain and concept known as artificial intelligence and concerned with the creation of intelligent machines resembling humans, more precisely, having qualities such as those of a human being, started to produce intelligent machines.

The disciplines implied by artificial intelligence are extremely various. Fields of knowledge such as Mathematics, Psychology, Philosophy, Logic, Engineering, Social Sciences, Cognitive Sciences and Computer Science are extremely important and closely interrelated are extremely important when it comes to artificial intelligence. All these fields and sciences contribute to the creation of intelligent machines that have a resemblance to human beings.

The application areas of artificial intelligence are extremely various such as Robotics, Soft Computing, Learning Systems, Planning, Knowledge Representation and Reasoning, Logic Programming, Natural Language Processing, Image Recognition,

Image Understanding, Computer Vision, Scheduling, Expert Systems and more others.

The field of artificial intelligence has recorded a rapid and spectacular evolution since 1956, researchers achieving great successes in creating intelligent machines capable of partially doing what human beings are able to do.

Obviously, researchers have encountered and still encounter several problems in simulating human intelligence. An intelligent machine must have a number of characteristics and must correspond to some particular standards. For instance, the human being is able of solving a problem faster by using mainly intuitive judgments rather than conscious judgments.

Another aspect that researchers have considerably analyzed was the knowledge representation which refers to the knowledge about the world that intelligent machines must have in order to solve problems such as objects or categories of objects, properties of objects, relations between objects, relations such as those between causes and effects, circumstances, situations etc.

Moreover, another challenge for researchers in the field of artificial intelligence refers to the fact that intelligent machines must be able to plan the problems that need to be solved, to set a number of goals that must be achieved, to be able to make choices and predict actions, they must be able learn, to understand the human languages and to display emotions and be able to understand and predict the behavior of the others.

Artificial intelligence is an extremely challenging and vast field of knowledge which poses many questions and generates many controversies but also solves many problems that technology and industry are confronting with today and may offer many answers in the future.

www.ingramcontent.com/pod-product-compliance
Lightning Source LLC
LaVergne TN
LVHW051344050326
832903LV00031B/3735